RESEARCHING YOUR

Colonial

NEW ENGLAND
ANCESTORS

RESEARCHING YOUR

Colonial

NEW ENGLAND
ANCESTORS

PATRICIA LAW HATCHER, FASG

Ancestry

Library of Congress Cataloging-in-Publication Data

Hatcher, Patricia Law.
Researching your colonial New England ancestors / by Patricia Law Hatcher.
   p. cm.
Includes bibliographical references and index.
ISBN 1-59331-299-7 (pbk. : alk. paper)
1. New England—Genealogy—Handbooks, manuals, etc. 2. New England—History. I. Title.
F3.H28 2006
929'.1072074—dc22

2006023564

First Printing 2006
10 9 8 7 6 5 4 3 2 1

Printed in the United States of America.

Contents

Introduction

We conduct genealogical research in reverse—from the present to the past. If our research goes well, at some point we may find ourselves crossing a significant research boundary, from doing *federal* research (after the Revolution) to doing *colonial* research (before the Revolution). Because geographical boundaries did not change when colonies became states, many researchers do not consciously expect to find differences when crossing this research boundary, but there are significant variances, especially in understanding the records and the environment in which they were created.

This book is intended as an introduction to finding your ancestor in colonial New England. It assumes that you have arrived in the colonial period through sound genealogical research and that you are familiar with basic records, repositories, and research techniques. Therefore, it focuses on what might be different about research in the colonial period. It does not repeat basics of genealogical research.

The settlement of New England, its religious and political controversies, its wars, and its relationship with the native populations have been discussed in hundreds of books and articles, some of which are indicated in the Resources section. The Background section presents an overview of those topics and provides an historical framework oriented toward genealogists.

The researcher will encounter a myriad of nonstandard records and sources in colonial research. Especially during the early colonial period, understanding the history and background, which define the environment in which records were created, is often more important than a reference catalog of records.

Many elements of life were different for our colonial ancestors. Of primary significance is that they were English, not American. The English crown could—and did—dictate colonial affairs. Our wars were European wars. The governing entities did not merely regulate religion and franchise (voting), but controlled them.

Colonial Americans were significantly less ethnically diverse than Americans in the nineteenth century, and this diversity varied from colony to colony. The mass of migration that created what we think of as the great American melting pot came after the colonial period ended. Any migration is said to have a "push" and a "pull." In the colonial period, the push was often greater than the pull. In effect, people were more likely to be emigrating *from* Europe, usually England, than to be immigrating *to* the American colonies.

The individual American colonies were far from homogenous. There were significant differences—both individual and regional—among them. The founding of each colony established, in effect, a personality for the colony. In turn, this personality directed governmental structure by determining not only jurisdictional entities and levels, but also such things as which actions and records were public and which were private. Each colony attracted different types of settlers who left their own stamp on the personality of the colony. The Background section of this book discusses the founding basis for each colony, the governmental structure, and the types of public and private records you can expect to find.

It is important to understand the differences among the colonies in order to understand your ancestors' lives and records correctly. Throughout this volume you will find some comparisons to other colonies, especially when pointing out differences.

We are hobbled by a familiar phrase, "the thirteen original colonies." The number comes from those ratifying the Constitution. There were, however, many more colonies or colonial settlements than that; these are described in the Background section.

From the European point of view—the point of view of our ancestors—"the colonies" were not confined to the outlines of those thirteen. Islands, from the failed Puritan experiment at Providence Island to the profitable plantations in Bermuda and the West Indies, were important. To the north lay what we think of as "Canada," another country. But in the colonial period, the Maritime Provinces of Canada were, like the American colonies, simply other British colonies. This book is not going to cover research beyond our current boundaries, but the researcher needs to remember that Europeans and American colonists had a more flexible view of the western hemisphere and that family relationships and vital events may have occurred outside of our current borders.

The Resources section lists standard references. When reference is made in the text to a publication not in the Resource list, the bibliographic details are given in endnotes.

CHAPTER ONE

Background

ollowing Columbus's landfall in the western hemisphere in 1492, European adventurers and fishermen visited America for more than a century. These ventures, however, did not result in permanent, family-oriented settlements.

The Spanish, chasing first the dream of a waterway to the East Indies and then the dream of riches from gold, explored the lower south of what became colonial America and the more westward region of the continent. Although we memorized the names of these explorers in history class, their primary influence was not in establishing permanent settlements, but in staking a Spanish (Catholic) presence through forts and missions that would help define the southern limits of the English American colonies.

To protect the riches carried in their ships from Mexico to Spain, the Spaniards established colonies in East Florida. Thus, St. Augustine, founded in 1565, is the oldest surviving European settlement in America, although the colonies of East Florida and West Florida did not become what we think of as American until 1763 when they were joined together and came under English rule.

Beginning its explorations a few decades later than Spain, France explored the St. Lawrence and Mississippi river valleys and their tributaries. Like the Spanish, they were seeking a waterway to the East Indies, but they soon recognized economic value in the furs found in what is now Canada, and its adjoining regions. Their settlements were generally small and short-lived, although the outpost established at Quebec in 1608 persevered as a stronghold from which the French harassed the New England frontier during most of the colonial era.

The first permanent English settlement in present-day America is considered to be Jamestown in 1607. The next settlement was that of the Pilgrims at Plymouth in 1620, with the major Puritan migration commencing with the Winthrop fleet of 1630.

Henry Hudson sailed up the Hudson River in 1608, seeking a waterway to China. New York was settled by the Dutch at New Amsterdam (now Manhattan) in 1624, and became English in 1664, while settlement of Lord Baltimore's Maryland began in 1633. Swedish settlements were established in Delaware in the 1640s.

Profile of Immigrants

The nature of immigration to America from England varied over time and among the colonies. For example, London departure records from 1635 describe almost five thousand persons bound for the New World by name, age, and ship. In *Migration and Origins of the English Atlantic World* (see "Resources"), Alison Games analyzed these lists demographically. She found that 41% were headed to Virginia, 24% to New England, and 35% to Barbados, Bermuda, St. Kitts, and Providence Island (an island off Nicaragua founded by Puritans).

An often-neglected element of the colonial experience is the importance of the islands of Bermuda and the West Indies. Columbus landed in the West Indies. The first major colonial settlement in the western hemisphere was established the following year on the island of Hispañola (present-day Haiti and Dominican Republic). Several European nations claimed territory and established settlements in Bermuda and the West Indies that became important points of trade and a connection between Europe and the American colonies. A significant percentage of emigration from England was to these islands. It isn't uncommon to find colonial American settlers who first settled in the islands or who had family members there. Many English businessmen had sugar plantations there or conducted brisk trade with the islands.

Games also found a significant difference in the composition of the passengers based on their destinations. Of the travelers to New England, thirty-nine percent were female, but of those to Virginia, less than fourteen percent were female. Less than eight percent of the passengers on the ships bound for the islands were female.

The reason for this becomes apparent when one examines the passengers' ages. The passengers to New England were similar in ages to the overall mix in England, except that there were—understandably—fewer elderly persons and more between the ages of fifteen and twenty-four. To Virginia and the islands, however, more than two-thirds of the passengers were between the ages of fifteen and twenty-four.

Clearly, the emphasis in New England was for family migration, in contrast to the young, single men going to the South and the islands. This can also be seen in the obvious family groupings on the port lists. When a more in-depth study is done using Anderson's *Great Migration* series (see "Resources"), extended families of dissimilar surnames are revealed as traveling together, as are sequential family migrations in which not all family members traveled together.

Plymouth Colony

The colonial settlements at Jamestown and at Plymouth, although very different in nature, had identical roots. A royal charter was granted in 1606 for the Virginia Company (at that time all of English America was called Virginia, for the Virgin Queen Elizabeth) to two groups of businessmen—one from London and the other from Plymouth. These companies planned to colonize, with the settlers working for the company, which would reap the profits of their labors.

At the same time that the London Company was sending its ships to Jamestown, the Plymouth Company was sending settlers to Sagadahoc on the Kennebec River in the cold environs of present-day Maine. Sagadahoc failed, largely due to lack of leadership, but when the settlers returned to their homeland, the general perception was that they quit because the climate was too harsh, discouraging other attempts.

The company never financed another settlement. Instead, the Plymouth Company reorganized as the Council of New England and granted land to the group of separatists we know as the Pilgrims. New England was apparently still seen as a hostile environment, because the land granted to the group in 1620 was in Virginia, purchased from the London Company. Hostile weather, however, forced them ashore at Plymouth, where they remained. They were joined by others of their group in 1621 and 1623. Originally, the settlers were to work communally for the company for seven years, but this plan was not successful. In 1623, the land was divided among the families, after which the colony became self-supporting and paid back the Council.

When the Pilgrims realized that their voyage was not going to conclude in the planned location, the group met on shipboard and drafted and signed the Mayflower Compact, in which they agreed to form and abide by a self-governing group, based on their understanding of congregational church structure.

When the time came to allocate land to individuals, a similar theory was used. With an understanding that the land must support the household, they allocated an acre of land per person. In the meantime, however, the community continued to hold its livestock in common. In 1627 this was reorganized, with the livestock still held in common, but by much smaller groups of individuals. The documents that describe these changes—dividing the land and dividing the cattle—tell us as genealogists about the individuals in the community and are the equivalent of a early census.

As the settlement at Plymouth grew, expansion was first along Cape Cod Bay, with Duxbury established in 1632 and Scituate in 1633. Eventually settlements would dot Cape Cod and extend to the islands of Nantucket and Martha's Vineyard, although the latter was under New York administration until 1695. Expansion to inland locations began with the founding of Taunton in 1639, Rehoboth in 1645, and Middleborough in 1669. The colony existed as a separate entity until 1692 when it was united with Massachusetts Bay Colony.

The Plymouth experience was indicative of several elements of the New England personality—governance at a local level, the application of the principles of religion to government, and an emphasis on the common good.

Massachusetts Bay Colony

The major wave of immigrants to New England—the Puritans—had both similarities to and differences from the Pilgrims. They, too, disagreed with the structure and rules of the Church of England. But they wanted to change the church, not separate from it. The Puritans originally planned to settle at Naumkeag, the Indian name for Salem, but they quickly saw that Boston was a superior choice.

We usually refer to the Puritan immigration that began with the Winthrop fleet in 1630 and lasted through that decade as the Great Migration. John Winthrop intended to create his vision of a "city on a hill" that could serve as a model for Puritan religion and government, far from the corrupting influences in England. He had no plans to encourage independence or dissension. Massachusetts Bay would be a thoroughly Puritan colony. The original autocratic model was soon adjusted. Freemen, who were church members recognized by the General Court (the governing entity of Massachusetts Bay), would choose representatives to the General Court. The requirement that freemen had to be members of a recognized church inextricably linked religious and political governance.

Historians shape our image of history, and our understanding of historical events has changed throughout time as popular attitudes have changed and as new research has emerged. If you remember from your school days something about the Pilgrims and Puritans and religious freedom, this would be a good time to forget it. When their own idea of how the Church of England should function was forbidden, portions of the group that would settle Plymouth left England for Leyden in Holland, where they could worship as they pleased. Once on the other side of the Atlantic, they hoped to continue their insularity. The Puritans weren't any more tolerant, however. Having established themselves in Massachusetts, they were determined to define and maintain both church and state according to their ideal model.

Expanding Settlement

Two major influences drove the settlement of new towns—a growing population and differences of opinion. The early New England settlements were small, geographically focused, and easily described: the separatists in Plymouth Colony, the Puritans in Massachusetts Bay, and the fishing settlements along the northern coast.

In 1633, William Laud was elevated to the position of Archbishop of Canterbury, and the persecution of English Puritans escalated. Soon, those who had until then been able to pursue their Puritan beliefs quietly in England found it necessary to relocate. They did so in great numbers.

In the interim between Winthrop's sailing and this turning point, Puritan theology on both sides of the Atlantic had developed along slightly different paths, with individual ministers having their own interpretations. This created differences of opinion that seemed anything but minor to the various groups trying to coexist in the Massachusetts Bay Colony theocracy.

England's economy was heavily dependent on textiles. At the time of the Great Migration, the industry was in serious decline. Thus, many who tolerated Puritanism, if they were not strong Puritans themselves, joined the migration in hopes of finding better economic circumstances. These families and individuals were not allied to a particular minister, as many Puritans were. There were many youthful, single immigrants who married soon after arrival, extending the family web. Thus, it is difficult and risky to assign migration motives to specific individuals, even those who are seen moving with a particular leader.

Anne (Marbury) Hutchinson and her involvement in what is known as the Antinomian Controversy became a focal point of many of these differences. As Puritan divines argued about Hutchinson, additional conflicts surfaced. This led to a major outflux from the earlier settlements around Massachusetts Bay, establishing settlements far from the reach of the Boston magistrates—in Connecticut, New Haven, Rhode Island, and New Hampshire. These migrations were not the uncoordinated moves of individuals that are seen in the middle and southern colonies, but organized relocations of groups of like-minded people, usually centered around a religious leader.

Planting Towns and Settling the Frontier

Unlike the middle and southern colonies, New Englanders did not move out into the frontier wilderness and select their own land. Instead, as the need became apparent, leaders—whether dissenters or part of the establishment—determined the best location for planting a new town.

At first, new settlements clustered near Boston and along Massachusetts Bay. As the New England population grew, new towns were planted further inland and along river valleys. The Puritan leaders—even those who moved out of the Boston area due to theological differences—believed in an ordered structure. Although new colonies and towns differed from Winthrop's vision in details, the method and organization was similar. Some theologically prompted settlements were more restrictive and some were less restrictive, but each reflected a desire to establish a church-state model. Only in Rhode Island were the two separate.

The religious foundations of the New England town model said that the community was more important than its individuals. It was designed for the common good, so New England proprietors, who were town residents, behaved differently than the royal-charter proprietors of the middle and southern colonies. There were approximately one hundred proprietors or more in a town.

The proprietors determined a good location for the town lots, the best pasture land, growing land, marsh land, and so on. They determined how many families in the town were approved residents and thus eligible for land. The land was surveyed, subdividing each type of land into a sufficient number of portions for the families or designating it as common land. Some land was specified for community use: roads, church, school, burying ground, and communal grazing. Parcels were allocated for future growth.

The land was then distributed in a communal way. The settlers drew for their lots, in what the records often called "the first division." Each family might get one town lot and one meadow lot. Some towns determined the size of the lot based on the size of the family. Things weren't necessarily exactly equal; sometimes the town leaders got better or larger lots.

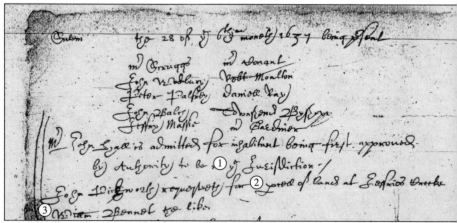

Towns were responsible for admitting inhabitants and granting land to them. Notice the use of (1) the thorn (as in ye) and (2) the per symbol, both common in colonial handwriting; (3) the bar over the L's in Willm indicates that letters are omitted.

When the time came to dispose of additional land ("the second division"), it was once again an orderly, controlled process, in which the land reserved for future growth was surveyed into lots and the drawing done according to the needs determined by the town leaders.

The first inland towns were Concord in 1635, Sudbury in 1639, Reading in 1644, and Andover in 1646.

The frontier settlements, no matter how orderly their planting, were still exposed to attacks by the French (based in Canada) and the Indians (incited by the French) during most of the colonial period. Many of these settlements suffered greatly, as they were burned out, with many casualties incurred and captives taken. There were more than a thousand captives. Some died or were killed while in captivity, some were redeemed, but some remained in Indian villages or Canadian settlements, becoming part of those communities, marrying, and having children. Demos's *Unredeemed Captive* is a popular narrative about one captive from Deerfield. Haefeli and Sweeney's recent *Captors and Captives* attempts a balanced approach. Coleman's *New England Captives Carried to Canada between 1677 and 1760 during the French and Indian Wars* is a more encyclopedic work, providing excellent and readable background on the frontier wars. Calder's *Colonial Captivities, Marches, and Journeys* contains a collection of journals and letters.[1]

Thus, we see a slow but uneven expansion outward from the coastal settlements. There were periodic contractions as settlements were abandoned, or nearly so, following attacks. This was especially widespread during King Philip's war, from 1675 to 1677.

Connecticut and New Haven Colonies

Connecticut was originally two separate colonies with separate charters. Both were founded by religious leaders who disagreed with Winthrop's interpretation of Puritanism, although in opposite ways.

Reverend Thomas Hooker led a group in 1636 from Cambridge to the fertile Connecticut River valley, where they established the town of Hartford. They were soon joined in the valley at Wethersfield by a group from Watertown and at Windsor by a group from Dorchester.

The Connecticut River was an important influence in the subsequent settlement of New England, both because of its excellent farm land and because it was a natural migration route. It extended from its mouth on Long Island Sound at Saybrook northward to Wethersfield, Windsor, and Hartford in Connecticut, and then to Springfield in Massachusetts, which was settled that same year. The river continues almost straight north and is the boundary of present-day New Hampshire and Vermont. Therefore, you may find many colonial residents of western Massachusetts, New Hampshire, and Vermont whose roots lie in Connecticut.

Theophilus Eaton and Reverend John Davenport led a group from London in 1637. Although Winthrop offered them a choice of several attractive places to settle, they declined, preferring to be as far removed from Winthrop and the new governor, Sir Henry Vane, as possible. They remained for a time in Boston until the Indian problems known as the Pequot War were resolved. The merchants in the group were especially interested in the commercial potential of Long Island Sound and selected what is now New Haven, Connecticut.

The New Haven founders also included a number of people already present in Massachusetts who were equally anxious to distance themselves from Massachusetts Bay Colony control. Calder's *New Haven Colony* and *Letters of John Davenport*[2] offer the most thorough treatments of this initial settlement, although her statements of origin for individuals should not be accepted without investigation. The group also included Reverend Peter Prudden and his followers, who soon after founded the town of Milford.

In addition to migration up the Connecticut River, there was migration from Connecticut to New Jersey and back and forth to Long Island.

Rhode Island

Roger Williams, who became the founder of Rhode Island, changed his religious convictions more than any other well-known figure. Having been a minister in the Anglican church, he settled at Salem as a Puritan, then at Plymouth as a Separatist, then returned to Salem. He objected to the strong control the magistrates of Massachusetts Bay Colony exercised over religious matters and also challenged their right to convey the land their royal charter gave them, for which they had not obtained title from the Indians.

In 1636, Williams found it necessary to depart Salem to avoid arrest. After wintering with the Indians, he founded Providence. He based the Rhode Island colony on principles that were more egalitarian than had been seen—or even suggested—anywhere else in New England. During his years in Rhode Island, he would be influenced by the Baptists, but would later join the sect known as Seekers.

Anne (Marbury) Hutchinson had come to New England as a follower of John Cotton. An intelligent and gifted woman, she was among many in Boston who met and discussed the Bible and sermons. However, she began to hold beliefs that were distinctly at odds with the ministers in Massachusetts Bay Colony, although she had popular support among the people. Ultimately she was arrested, tried, imprisoned, and banished, going first to Rhode Island and settling Portsmouth in 1638. She ended up with her large family in New York, where most of them were killed by Indians.

The more welcoming attitude of Rhode Island didn't mean that the old patterns were dropped. The third town, Newport, was founded in 1639 by an unhappy group from Portsmouth. The fourth town, Warwick, was settled by the contentious Samuel Gorton, who couldn't fit in at either Portsmouth or Providence.

Unlike Plymouth and Massachusetts Bay, which had central colony governments, the four Rhode Island towns governed themselves until 1644, when Williams obtained a royal charter uniting them.

Rhode Island is known for its liberal governance and most especially for its religious tolerance. Particularly irksome to its larger neighbors was the fact that it accepted Quakers. Rhode Island also had a significant Baptist settlement, particularly in the west.

It is not surprising, since Narragansett Bay cuts deeply into the center of the colony, that much of its enterprise would be related to the sea.

Early Northern New England

The settlement of northern New England had its roots in villages meant to service the vessels working the fishing grounds along the coast. A succession of confusing and overlapping grants by the Plymouth Company (later the Council of New England) were the basis for tiny settlements at the Isles of Shoals, Monhegan, Dover, Strawberry Bank (Portsmouth), and Rye. Like the fishing villages southward at Cape Ann and Naumkeag (Salem), they were locations for drying and salting fish that was then sold primarily to Catholic Spain. Ironically, although a rich variety of seafood was available, the English considered fish and shellfish—even lobster—to be food of last resort.

New Hampshire

As inflexible religious policies prompted groups to distance themselves from Boston and the seat of the Massachusetts Bay Colony, those moving northward settled Exeter and Hampton in 1638. Leaders included the Reverend John Wheelwright, husband of Anne Hutchinson's sister. The land and climate were not well suited to agriculture, but the forests supplied masts and timber for shipbuilding, and, augmented by the fur trade, the settlements survived and new ones were established.

These New Hampshire towns were under the nominal governance of Massachusetts Bay Colony—as part of "Old Norfolk" County beginning in 1643—until 1679 when New Hampshire obtained its own charter.

About 1720, another group became a significant presence in New Hampshire when Scotch-Irish Presbyterians settled in the area around Londonderry, including the towns of Amherst, Bedford, and Goffstown.

The population in New Hampshire first spread outward from the Piscataqua River towns. As central Massachusetts became settled and expanded northward, New Hampshire gained residents, especially with the grants at Rindge and Jaffrey. At the end of the colonial period, families came up the Connecticut River and made settlements such as Acworth, which was established in 1768, along the western border.

Maine

Sir Ferdinando Gorges had a charter for the area from the Council of New England, but did nothing about it until his falling out with Massachusetts Bay, at which time the family actively sought confirmation of the charter that they had obtained in 1639. It remained in the family until purchased by Massachusetts in 1691.

Maine remained part of Massachusetts until after the Revolutionary War. As with New Hampshire, Maine's settlements were primarily coastal. It had some settlement on its western border from towns in south central New Hampshire. Its forests provided a business foundation for the small settlements along its rivers.

Vermont

Vermont was largely unsettled until the early 1750s. Although it was not an original colony, it had settlements in the colonial period, governed either by New Hampshire or New York. Settlement became more concentrated when migration up the Connecticut River led to the establishing of a number of towns across the river from New Hampshire, with many of the families coming from towns in Connecticut. Additionally, there was migration from New York on its western border. These western Vermonters often saw themselves as New Yorkers, not New Englanders, and their county-level records until 1777 are in New York counties.

The New England Confederation

Although each New England colony functioned separately, they all saw a need to have some cooperation, especially to defend against attack from the French and the Dutch and to settle disputes between colonies. In 1643, Massachusetts Bay, Plymouth, New Haven, and Connecticut—but not the outcast Rhode Island—formed the New England Confederation.

The Andros Regime

In 1684, mainly because of its independent attitude, the charter of Massachusetts Bay Colony was revoked. This caused a great deal of uncertainly, since it threw such things as the court system and land transactions into question. It also ushered in one of the unhappiest periods in New England, when Sir Edmund Andros arrived in 1686, appointed by James II to begin governing the Dominion of New England (to which were added New York and New Jersey). His autocratic policies and arrogant ways went against the independent New England character, angering almost everyone except Rhode Island, which Andros largely ignored. He began by demanding that Connecticut's charter be given to him. Legend has it that the charter was hidden away in a hollow tree—the Charter Oak. In 1689, when news reached the colony that James was no longer on the throne, there was open revolt in Boston and Andros was taken prisoner and sent back to England.

Late-Colonial Settlements

In the latter third of the seventeenth century, a new type of settlement developed that was quite different from the controlled planting of religiously-orthodox satellite towns overseen by proprietors. Pressure from profit-seeking merchants and the revival of old grants in

New Hampshire and Massachusetts led to the approved establishment of towns in which speculators could acquire land.

In a proactive attempt to fortify their claim in their boundary squabble with New Hampshire, in 1735 and 1736 Massachusetts deliberately laid out a number of towns in the area claimed by New Hampshire and granted land within them. They made grants, known as the Narragansett townships, to the soldiers who fought in King Philip's War and to their heirs, as most of the soldiers were dead by then. Two of the towns were in Massachusetts: Narragansett #2 (Westminster) and Narragansett #6 (Templeton). Three were in New Hampshire: Narragansett #3 (Amherst or Sowhegan West), Narragansett #4 (Goffstown), and Narragansett #5 (Bedford or Sowhegan East). Two were in what is now Maine: Narragansett #1 (Buxton) and Narragansett #7 (Gorham). Lists of soldiers and claimants are in Bodge's *Soldiers in King Phillip's War*.[3]

Massachusetts also made grants to the soldiers in the 1690 expedition to Canada and their heirs. The companies from Dorchester, Ipswich, Rowley, and other Massachusetts towns each received the grant of a township. The towns were descriptively named Dorchester Canada (now Ashburnham, Massachusetts), Ipswich Canada (now Winchendon, Massachusetts) and Rowley Canada (also referred to as Monadnock, now principally Rindge and Jaffrey, New Hampshire).

Having broken away from the orderly structure of the early New England model, the Massachusetts Court quickly created several dozen more towns in Massachusetts, New Hampshire, and Maine. It then began the sale of town sites, and by 1762 all of Massachusetts was defined as towns. This created a distinct flip-flop in the dynamics of settlement. Initially, towns were established when people needed land. Now, towns and land were available—it was people who were needed. In turn, this ended any idea of religious orthodoxy. In particular, it probably accelerated the immigration of the Scotch-Irish[4] into New England.

Migration, Boundaries, and Land Claims

The majority of migration and expanding settlement was on a regional basis. Until the decades before the American Revolution, most settlers moved within the New England, mid-Atlantic, or Southern region in which they had first settled. However, there was trade, commerce, and even investment between one port and another and with the West Indies. Thus, in merchant and seaman families, you may find a familial outpost or marriage alliance in a surprisingly distant location.

In New England, there was also a certain amount of migration to and from New York and New Jersey, particularly in the areas around Long Island Sound and along the border that New York shared with Connecticut, Massachusetts, and Vermont.

In 1638, Massachusetts surveyed its borders with New Hampshire (along the Merrimack River), with Connecticut, and with Plymouth Colony.

New Hampshire and Massachusetts disagreed through a major portion of the colonial period over their common boundary line, which was finally settled by royal decree in 1740, although protested for several more years by Massachusetts.

The boundary line between western Rhode Island and eastern Connecticut was under dispute in the seventeenth century (largely because the surveyors from Rhode Island arbitrarily decided to move the generally accepted line some distance to the west), but residents of Voluntown, Connecticut, as well as other areas claimed by Rhode Island, were quite certain where they lived, so it does not usually affect your research.

In 1747, the present-day eastern border of Rhode Island was established when Massachusetts ceded Bristol, Cumberland, Little Compton, Tiverton, and Warren to Rhode Island. County-level records prior to this date are in Bristol County, Massachusetts.

Connecticut—through the Susquehanna Company—claimed land in the Wyoming Valley of the upper Susquehanna River in Pennsylvania. It was settled by Connecticut residents in the late colonial period.

What It Means to Be Colonial

The word "colonial" should be a constant reminder that America was not an independent entity, but was a colony of England. During the colonial period we were for the most part under the governance of the English crown, except for the significant Dutch control in the early middle colonies.

Rulers wanted colonies to be beneficial to the crown. In particular, they wanted financial usefulness through business ventures and taxation. They also perceived colonies as a way to reward backers without adversely affecting their own pocketbooks. They accomplished this through granting of proprietary land rights and appointment to political office.

Additionally, colonies could be a convenience: an overflow valve for relieving overcrowding, religious unrest, and economic problems, and as a place to send convicted criminals and debtors.

As a distanced part of England, America followed English models of law, governance, and social activities. But at the same time, America was unique because of its frontier border, a shifting area in which those laws, governmental structures, and social activities were often impractical, inconvenient, and immaterial.

The frontier, with its unsettled lands, attracted individuals and families from the more-settled colonial areas, especially in the second and third generations as available land became scarce. It also attracted new settlers from Europe. These newer settlers often came from different localities and for different reasons than the colony founders, requiring adjustments in attitude for leaders and government.

English Wars and American Conflicts

The colonial military experience in New England began with several significant English-Indian conflicts. As an English colony, the American colonists found themselves involved in the major conflicts that took place on the American continent.

- The Pequot War (1636–1637) was sparked by the exodus from Boston of disgruntled Puritans who settled in what is now Connecticut. The Pequots occupied land on Long Island Sound between the Monhegans and the Narragansetts. They were not on good terms with either tribe. After the Pequots had captured or killed about twenty English settlers, the other tribes helped the English attack them in a single event in which almost the entire Pequot population was killed. The Indian tribes regularly fought with each other, but rarely killed, usually taking captives instead, whom they sold as slaves or adopted into their own tribes. This bloody battle defined for the Indians the English style of warfare and ushered in four decades without major conflict.

- King Philip's War (1675–1676) in New England was devastating in both human and economic terms for the Indians and the English settlers. Both groups, as a percentage of the whole, suffered greater losses than in any other American conflict. Expansion had pushed the English settlements into Indian lands, displacing the Indians. It was clear to the Wampanoag chief Metacom (known to the English as King Philip) that the trend would only accelerate, so he attacked. Especially vulnerable were the settlements on the frontiers. The towns of Brookfield, Deerfield, Groton, Middleborough, Northfield, Lancaster, Providence, Springfield, and Warwick were destroyed or severely crippled.[5]

- Lovewell's War (1722–1726), also known as Governor Dummer's War or the Three-Years War, was fought in northern New England against Indians.

- The War of Jenkin's Ear (1739–1743) began at sea in an incident with the Spanish.

Localized skirmishes with the Indians throughout the colonial period made life on the frontier difficult.

America was also involved in the four major English wars of the colonial period. New England, because of the French possession of Canada, was the most severely impacted. However, all regions suffered from interference to shipping and the uncertainty of the outcome. In hindsight, we know that the British won each conflict, but at the time, such was not a foregone conclusion.

- King William's War (1689–1697), known in Europe as the War of the Palatinate, was fought by the French from Quebec, often using Indians as the striking force. In addition to targets in present-day

Voluntown, Connecticut, was one of several towns whose lands were given to veterans of vari *ous conflicts with the French and Indians. Those settlers were joined in the 1720s by Scotch-* *Irish Presbyterians fleeing conditions in Ireland.*

Canada, attacks were made against the frontier English settlements along the Great Lakes, in upstate New York, and in western and northern New England, particularly in Maine.

- Queen Ann's War (1702–1713), known in Europe as the War of Spanish Succession, affected two separate areas of the American colonies: the frontier of New England and the frontier of the lower South. France's allies were Spain and, once again, the Indians. This conflict was a reminder that our eastern border was an ocean. The fear of attack on the port of Charleston was constant. New England saw its share of sea-based attacks.

- King George's War (1744–1748), known in Europe as the War of Austrian Succession, had very little effect on the American colonies, except for attacks on frontier settlements in New York (with about 30 fatalities at Saratoga), New Hampshire, and Maine. A major contingent from Massachusetts sailed to—and eventually overtook—the French fort at Louisbourg, Cape Breton Island (today Nova Scotia). The colonies were much annoyed when England signed away this possession in the peace treaty—a justifiable attitude, especially when they had to turn around and win it back in the next war.

- French and Indian War (1754–1763), known in Europe as the Seven Years' War, began in America with the fight for French-occupied Fort Duquesne at present-day Pittsburgh, where George Washington's Virginia troops were defeated in his first military campaign, as were General Braddock's British troops. Indians from various tribes then began attacking frontier settlements, killing or capturing at least 700 pioneers in Pennsylvania, Maryland, and Virginia. There was significant American involvement—about half of all troops—in a war with many casualties. Most of the fighting was on the northern front. In 1756 the British lost forts Oswego and William Henry; in 1758 they lost Fort Ticonderoga, but took Frontenac and—finally— Fort Duquesne, leading the Indians to switch sides and support the English. In 1759, the British won Crown Point, Ticonderoga, and the critical Quebec. The war was effectively over in America when Montreal fell in 1760. The Treaty of Paris formally ended the French presence in North America. Spain ceded Florida to the British.

This effectively left the lands west of the Appalachian mountains and east of the Mississippi in English hands. But whose hands? Those of the Crown or those of the colonies who had grants that extended to the Pacific Ocean? The decision was to avoid the decision. The proclamation of 1763 closed off any trans-Appalachian settlement, reserving the land for the Indians. This established the colonial frontier at the eve of the American Revolution.

Demographics

Using federal government estimates for the colonial period,[6] we can see that the New England population grew from the initial band of Pilgrims and fishing settlements to almost a quarter of a million people near the end of the colonial period. Growth was steady but moderate—about the rate of normal population growth, indicating little immigration—from the conclusion of the Great Migration until the 1710s, when a steeper growth rate resulted from fresh immigration, spurred by conditions in Europe.

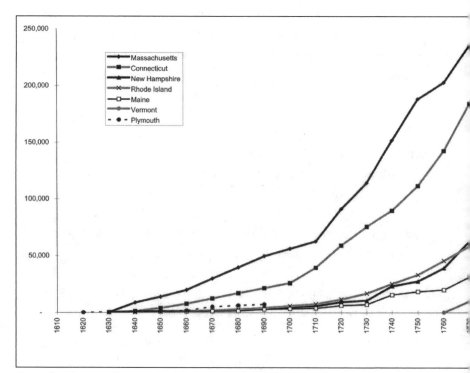

A graph indicating the growth of the New England population throughout the colonial period.

Religion

Church records before and after the American Revolution are basically the same. What is not the same is the status of churches. The beginning of the First Amendment to the Constitution states "Congress shall make no law respecting an establishment of religion, or prohibiting the free exercise thereof." It defined separation between church and state because separation did not exist during the colonial period. The exact condition varied between colonies and over time, ranging from a heavily controlled state church to government-defined tolerance.

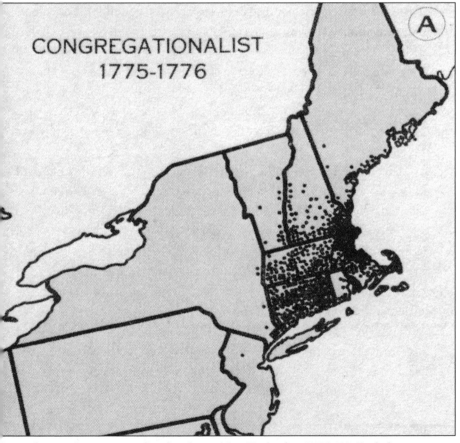

map showing Congregationalist churches in New England in 1775–76. Each dot represents e church. From Charles O. Paullin, Atlas of the Historical Geography of the United ates (Baltimore, MD: A. Hoen & Co., Inc., 1932).

25

About 1633, a change in Puritan theology began spreading, with a requirement that to become a full, professed, communing church member (a visible saint), an individual must make a structured confession of his or her religious odyssey and conversion experience. Not everyone did so. Thus, you may find a family in which only one spouse became a full, communing church member, although they both attended church services.

This requirement had a more long-reaching effect. As the second generation came of age, a problem became apparent, in that few of this generation could (or perhaps even cared to) produce this narration of saving grace, possibly because they had not witnessed the persecution of the Puritans in England. These children of communing members had been baptized as infants. Now, as adults, they were having children of their own. The theological question was, if a parent of a child had been baptized but never professed a conversion experience—and hence was not a fully participating member—could his or her children be baptized? The consensus was that the children could not be baptized, but this contributed further to the decline in church membership and influence.

The Half-Way Covenant, drawn up in 1662, allowed a baptized adult who was a fully participating member to have his or her children baptized, but neither the parents nor the children as they grew up would be able to take communion or to participate in church governance. Most, but not all, churches supported this compromise. For example, objection to its liberal terms was a primary motivating factor that led a group from Branford and New Haven, Connecticut, to establish the settlement at Newark, New Jersey.

The level of religious intolerance in Massachusetts Bay Colony was high until after the revocation of the colony's original charter and the issuance of the new charter in 1691, which explicitly decreed religious liberty to all Christians except Catholics.

Witchcraft

A belief in witchcraft and the devil's influence was widespread, held by both ministers and parishioners in England and in New England. The

inisters in the early Congregational churches wielded great influence. This is the pulpit in the ...reated church built for the filming of the movie about the Salem witchcraft hysteria of 1692, ...hree Sovereigns for Sarah, that aired on PBS.

colonies had seen several accusations of witchcraft. Some were casual talk, but others resulted in trials, especially in Connecticut in the mid-1600s.

The Salem witchcraft hysteria—which actually focused in Salem Farms, now Danvers—grew out of a variety of factors, including church politics, uncertainty over the loss of the colony charter, conflicts on the northern front, differences between town and farm, and hard feelings between neighbors. It was prolonged and promoted by the actions of the court of Oyer and Terminer. Several good studies have been published on the subject, and you should read them in order to gain perspective.[7]

The Great Awakening

A century after the earliest settlements, church membership and commitment in New England and elsewhere had become somewhat casual. The Great Awakening, led by charismatic preachers such as Jonathan Edwards, George Whitefield, Gilbert Tennent, and James Davenport prompted revivals of pietism from about 1734 through 1745. The main elements were evangelism and itinerancy (preaching by ministers, and occasionally by lay persons or ministers who did not meet the defined standard of education or approval), sermons with vivid descriptions of heaven and hell, enthusiastic conversions, and criticism of established ministers and church structure.

The movement began in the frontier settlements along the Connecticut River in Massachusetts, but spread to other colonies. It had its greatest effect among Calvinistic groups—Congregationalists in New England and Presbyterians in Pennsylvania. Because it broadly attacked the status quo—something that had not been seen earlier in colonial religions—the Great Awakening led to schisms within local churches, often with the formation of splinter congregations—breaking the one church per town model that had been a basis of New England life. In New England the two groups were called *Old Lights* and *New Lights*; in Pennsylvania the terms were *Old Side* and *New Side*.

Although as many as 50,000 conversions were said to have occurred, the commitment of many waned. The primary effect of the Great Awakening was the founding of new congregations and a change in mind-set that included the possibility of questioning religious structure, religious leaders, and the connection between church and state. The enthusiasm and energy of the new groups led to growth, particularly in Presbyterian and Baptist churches.

Denominations

New England was strongly Congregational because of its founding, but there were other denominations there.

- **Anglicans.** Anglicanism—the Church of England—was technically the official church of most of the colonies. However, the structure of individual colonies meant that it functioned as the state church only in Virginia, the Carolinas, Maryland, and Georgia; the official Anglican hierarchy was not established in the colonies.

- **Baptists.** The seventeenth-century concentration of Baptists was in Rhode Island, with many Welsh Baptists settling in Pennsylvania at the beginning of the eighteenth century. Baptists during the later colonial period were found throughout the colonies.

  New England residents with Baptist leanings were found in Salem, Lynn, Plymouth Colony, and Long Island in New York, but most ended up in Rhode Island where they were accepted. Swansea, Massachusetts, was founded in the 1660s by a group of Welsh Baptists who had originally been in Rehoboth in Plymouth Colony. In a well-publicized incident, Massachusetts Bay ordered fines and a whipping of Rhode Island residents who had journeyed to Lynn and held a service. Baptist congregations were not widespread, and even by 1740 there were only twenty-two Baptist churches in New England, half of them in Rhode Island.

- **Jews.** A Jewish synagogue was established in Newport, Rhode Island, in the 1700s.

- **Quakers.** Quakerism was popular and widespread. The heaviest concentration was obviously in Pennsylvania and the adjoining colonies of Delaware and New Jersey, but New England, New York (especially Long Island), Virginia, and North Carolina had many Quaker meetings.

Quakers were seriously persecuted by the Bay Colony, which in 1656 passed its first law against them. They were imprisoned, deported, banned, fined, and physically punished. In 1657, Rhode Island proclaimed that they could settle there. Four Quakers were hanged in Boston between 1658 and 1661. English Quakers appealed to Charles II, who ordered Massachusetts to send imprisoned Quakers to England for trial and to moderate their persecutions. In general, New England Quaker records have not been abstracted or published. Most are at the Rhode Island Historical Society, which has microfilm of the others.[8]

- **Scotch-Irish Presbyterians (Ulster Scots).** The Scottish population in Ulster (Northern Ireland) were Presbyterians, governed by England, which enacted several onerous economic and religious restrictions in the mid-eighteenth century. It has been said that as a result half of the million Presbyterians in Ulster emigrated to America beginning in the second decade of the eighteenth century.

The Scotch-Irish had a reputation for being loners who preferred isolation, lived on the frontier, and moved when they could see the smoke from another cabin. They certainly were comfortable settling the frontier, far from the close oversight of government (not unsurprising given their experience in Ireland), but many were happy to remain on the land they had cleared and become landowners, especially if a Presbyterian church had been established in the area.

The Scotch-Irish settlement at Londonderry is well-known, but there were Ulster Scots in many places in New England. Some were farther north in Maine, others spread westward from Worcester, Massachusetts, and some moved farther south to Milford and Voluntown in Connecticut. If there were sufficient numbers, they usually organized a church and called a Presbyterian minister, but the prevalence of the Congregational churches—which had the same Calvinistic roots—prevented them from becoming the significant presence they were in the middle colonies and the South.

Commerce, Trade, and Occupations

The colonies produced a variety of goods desired in England. The forests of the American colonies produced several types of lumber. They served as the basis for shipbuilding that further increased trade. Iron deposits, usually in the form of bog iron, were important assets where they were found. Intercolony trade was restricted, and trade with countries other than England was banned during much of the colonial period, but both occurred. There was extensive trade with Bermuda and the West Indies, which traded sugar, molasses, and rum for wood and other American products.

The fishing grounds of New England supplied fish primarily to the Catholic countries in continental Europe, but the rivers and streams were rich trapping grounds for beaver to supply the English fad for hats made from felt created from beaver fur.

Although New England was founded on a religious basis, business profit was a strong motivation directing colonists' actions. For example, the choice of the location for the Connecticut and New Haven settlements was strongly influenced by their appropriateness for trade.

In the seventeenth century, prices for goods and hourly wages were fixed, but by the eighteenth century, these has become impractical. England decreed to whom the colonies could sell goods and what they could export. These restrictions helped foment the dissatisfaction that formed a basis for the broad support of the American Revolution.

In some ways, there were two New England profiles—one turned toward the sea and one toward the land. Farmers in the short growing season of New England led a subsistence life, centered around livestock, a few crops, church, and—if they were on the frontier—concern about problems with the Indians and the French. They helped shape our image of the stoic New Englander. Along the coast, small towns supplied fishermen and ship building. Major towns focused on trade, were more sophisticated, and were concerned with threats from Europe by sea. They helped shape our image of the astute New England businessmen.

Transportation

Travel and transport in the colonial period was more likely to be by water than by road. The type of boat used depended on time, place, purpose, and nature of waterway. Shipbuilding quickly became an important industry for the colonies because England no longer had sufficient good timber. The colonists supplied shipyards in England with oak for planking and tall pine for masts, but they also built many vessels in the colonies, for export to England and for their own use, often adapting the style of Native American or European vessels.[9]

In much of New England, rivers were navigable only during the warmer months. Once ice locked them in, towns were effectively shut off from many of their visitors, supplies, and communication. Winter transportation was usually by sleds.

Roads were minimal, often just narrow paths from one town to the next, perhaps based on Indian trails. They were generally unmaintained, often muddy, rocky, and rutted. Many roads simply led to the nearest navigable waterway or ferry. In understanding our ancestors' movements, it is important to look as they did—to the water—rather than to roads.

Ethnicity, Servitude, and Slavery

The colonial period saw many individuals come as indentured servants (also called redemptioners) and as slaves. The living circumstances for both were often similar, but indenture was voluntary for the many who used it as a means to secure passage across the Atlantic and with it the potential for a better life. There were well-organized systems, with agents in England and on the continent and ship owners and captains who held the indenture during passage and sold it upon arrival to those seeking labor.

Typical indentures were four to seven years. Skilled craftsmen often received better terms, perhaps even a stipend or tools of their own. Indentured servitude was regulated beginning in 1661, and most received clothes and money upon completion of their term.

As shown in the following chart, on the eve of the Revolution the black population in New England was only 3% of the region; in the Middle colonies it was 13%, whereas in the South it was 43%.

The Middle colonies contained more non-English immigrants than their neighbors to either the north or south, with many family units. New Jersey and New York began as Dutch settlements. Delaware and New Jersey had Swedish settlements. Germans came primarily into the middle colonies, especially into New York and Pennsylvania. A significant number of the Germans moved near the end of the colonial period down the valley of Virginia and helped settle the back country. Almost all of the colonies saw Scotch-Irish (Ulster Scots) immigrants and many had Welsh.

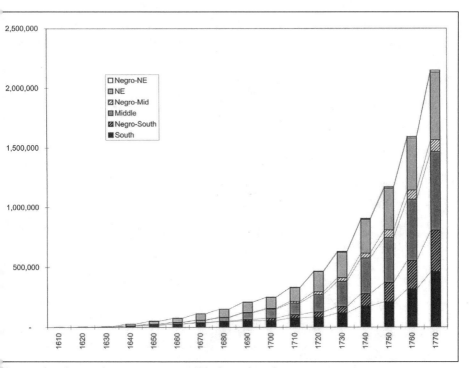

This graph indicates the concentration of blacks in the colonies.

You will find books about emigration, immigration, and settlement of specific ethic groups at your library, often in the history section rather than the genealogy section.[10] Dobson has written a large number of books listing Scots emigrants, which by default also list Scotch-Irish emigrants.[11]

Some immigrants came in identifiable clusters and settled near each other in areas whose names—such as Germantown, Germana, the Welsh Tract, Londonderry, or Swedesboro—flag their origins, but many were disbursed throughout the English population.

Usually we find the immigrant generation and the second generation associating primarily with others of the same ethnic group, but not isolating themselves. Thus, marriages were usually within the ethnic group, but business dealings were not. By the third generation, however, marriages in which the bride and groom are of differing ethnic origins were common.

In New England, there was very little slavery and much less servitude than in the South. This is because New England farms raised subsistence crops and livestock, rather than crops for sale and export. The small black population—almost all free—clustered in the cities and port towns. See Greene's *The Negro in Colonial New England* and Higginbotham's *In the Matter of Race* for additional information.[12]

Early Puritan immigrants often had servants with them. Many of these were young people who married soon after arrival, suggesting that they weren't indentured, but that it was more a case of sponsorship. The rest of the early arrivals were skilled at a craft. Soon, however, there was a broader class of servants, who are best known to us for their misdeeds, as they appear often in court records and are the subject of laws passed specifically to address their behavior.

New England was almost entirely English. The base population of New England was firmly established by the mid-1600s from the English Puritan migration and those who joined that migration because of the depressed textile industry in England. This resulted in a New England character that includes things as varied as styles of building construction, land use, diet, and the town as a basic governing unit.

Eighteenth-century immigrants to New England continued to come almost entirely from the British Isles. The analysis of surnames in the 1790 census—admittedly well after the end of the colonial period—identifies less than 1% of the population of New England as having German, Dutch, French, or Swedish origins. The percentage of Scotch, Scotch-Irish, and Irish combined was well below 10% in southern New England, but by 1790 was higher in Maine (16%), New Hampshire (14%), and Vermont (10%).

In addition to the Ulster Scots who settled around Londonderry, there were two groups of Scottish prisoners, from the Battle of Dunbar and from the Battle of Worcester, arriving in 1651 and 1652 respectively. Many of the first group went to work for the ironworks at Saugus (Lynn) and the works at Hammersmith and Braintree. Iron was an important element if the colonies were to be self-supporting. Hartley's *Ironworks on the Saugus* gives background on this early industry.[13] Many of the second group—for whom there is something of a list in the Suffolk

he gravestones of this couple in Lexington, Massachusetts, are tilted toward each other—peraps lovingly, but more likely as a result of the expanding and contracting ground during inter freezes. William is said to be one of the Scottish prisoners from the Battle of Worcester ho arrived in 1652.

35

County deeds[14]—were assigned to the Company of Undertakers (for establishing ironworks) in London, who sold most of the indentures, many to farmers.

Relationships with the Native Population

The relationships between the Europeans and the numerous Indian tribes who occupied the land when they arrived cannot be described simply. Explorers and settlers converted, befriended, hated, conquered, enslaved, expelled, and feared the Indians. They formed alliances with tribes or chieftains, bought land in friendly agreements, cohabited with native women, engaged in business and trade, brought decimating diseases, and—in the case of the non-English—incited the Indians as weapons against the English.

Newspapers and Broadsides

In the early colonial period, communication was very different than it was following the Revolution. The majority of America was ruled by England and the residents considered themselves Englishmen, not Americans. Their news was the news of England.

Printing presses, which we take for granted as mechanical devices, were considered by the Crown to be dangerous. The early colonists probably considered them irrelevant to their primary purpose of survival in a new world. When the first printing press was allowed in the colonies in 1638, it was overseen by Harvard College and produced broadsides, religious works, and useful books such as almanacs and law books.

Broadsides—printing on one side of a single sheet of paper—were used to convey "news" such as proclamations and ballads that related interesting events. The content was closely watched by the authorities.

The first regular newspaper in the colonies did not exist until 1704, nearly a century after the first permanent American settlement.

- In Massachusetts, a broadside containing news from 1689 was printed in Boston, but it failed after one issue. Consequently, the Boston Newsletter in 1704 is considered the first regular newspaper. It was followed by the Boston Gazette in 1719. Benjamin Franklin learned the printing business at the latter.

- Rhode Island was the second New England colony with a regular newspaper; the Rhode Island Gazette began publication in 1732.

- Connecticut's first newspaper was the Connecticut Gazette, founded in 1755. The Connecticut Courant was founded in 1764. It is now the Hartford Courant and is the longest continuously published newspaper in America.

- In the north, the New Hampshire Gazette was begun in 1756.

It wasn't until the two decades before the Revolutionary War that newspaper publishing began to proliferate. Many colonial newspapers were in publication for a relatively brief period.

What Colonial Americans considered news was not what we might expect. It was almost never local; the grapevine sufficed for that. There was a heavy emphasis on news from England and the continent, which was dependent on the arrival of ships carrying newspapers and other communications from England. News from other colonies was important, as were items of business.

Newspapers also carried a variety of advertising. Even in the colonial period, you can find ads for medicines that claimed to cure an incredible array of human ailments. Some newspapers offered literary content such as stories and poems. As time went on, some became more forward in taking political positions, although this was often done subtly or indirectly, so as not to bring about the closure of the paper.

Although deaths of important persons might be noticed, births and marriages would not. Local individuals were mentioned only as they related to business. Thus, you are likely to find the name of your ancestor only if he was offering items for sale, had detained wandering livestock, had letters at the post office, or had a servant or slave or wife who had run away—or if he or she *was* the runaway servant, slave, or wife.

As newspaper publishing spread, so did royal concern about it. The Crown sought some level of control through the Stamp Act of 1765. At that point, there were twenty-three newspapers operating in the colonies (about two dozen more had become defunct), in New Hampshire (1), Massachusetts (4), Connecticut (2), Rhode Island (2), New York (3), Pennsylvania (4, of which 2 were in German), Maryland (1), Virginia

(1), North Carolina (2), South Carolina (2), and Georgia (1). Only Delaware and New Jersey did not have a newspaper.

The Stamp Act decreed that all newspapers, books, and legal or official documents had to be printed on special stamped paper on which tax—a not insubstantial tax—had been paid. Additionally, advertisements would be taxed. It was probably anticipated that this would simultaneously bring income to the crown and put a damper on the increasingly political nature of some newspapers. Instead, it served as a focus for open rebellion.

In the six months between announcement and effect, the newspapers strongly attacked the act in a variety of ways. In the end, no American newspaper published on the stamped paper. Some suspended publication, some morphed into non-newspapers by removing the serial number or the name, and a few defiantly continued publication on normal paper. The act was repealed within a few months.[15]

Not all issues of all colonial newspapers survive. Almost all of what has survived has been put on microform by private companies. The Family History Library has only a few of these. They may be in college libraries or available on interlibrary loan. At present, early American newspapers at the American Antiquarian Society and elsewhere have been digitized, and the subscription-based "Early American Newspapers, 1690–1876" is available at many colleges, some public libraries, and as a benefit of membership in a few genealogical societies.

Several books abstracting genealogical information in newspapers include the colonial era, but the coverage is by no means comprehensive. These are listed in "Resources" under each colony.

Mail and the Post Office

Most communication was personal—and usually verbal, via the grapevine. Letters were often transported by friends who were traveling. However, there was somewhat of an organized postal system. Initially, postal contracts were royal contracts awarded to individuals. At the end of the 1600s, only Boston, New York, and Philadelphia had such contracts, with service to a few nearby settlements and those along the roads connecting the three towns.

The Post Office Act of 1711 changed the system, making the postmaster a royal appointment, rather than a private charter, which helped expand and improve postal service, especially in the southern colonies where settlement was dispersed.

There was a close link during the early eighteenth century between the mail and newspapers. Lists of letters waiting to be collected were published in newspapers. In several instances the postmaster was the printer of the newspaper. Newspapers were carried to other towns by the same riders who carried the mail.

As already mentioned, roads were not good. In fact, they were awful. News, whether contained in letters or newspapers, traveled slowly. Winter and rain further slowed the post riders.

The Revolutionary War created a difficult situation in the rebelling colonies because the postal service was a function of the English government. Some private postal delivery services had been established. The Continental Congress took over one such service in 1775, appointing Benjamin Franklin, who had been the crown's Deputy Postmaster General from 1752 until 1774, as the first Postmaster General of what would become the United States.

Education

The educational system in the early colonies was, not unsurprisingly, modeled on the English system, with three levels. Basic reading, writing, and ciphering were the responsibility of the family. Some children learned from parents, some attended classes, and some learned from their master in an apprenticeship. Girls were not excluded from this level of learning. The next level, for boys who showed both promise and interest, was grammar school (Latin school), where the entire focus was on learning Latin, with a bit of Greek.

There were significant differences among the colonies in their attitude toward education. In New England, education was considered a positive attribute. The South, on the other hand, viewed comprehensive education for other than the upper class to be dangerous. Young men from well-to-do families generally were sent back to England for schooling. The diversity of the middle colonies led to equally diverse attitudes toward education, influenced by ethic groups, religious groups, and their neighbors to the north and south.

Nine colleges were established in English colonial America—four in New England, four in the middle colonies, and one in the South.

- Harvard—Cambridge, Massachusetts. 1636.
- William and Mary—Williamsburg, Virginia. 1693.
- Yale—Saybrook (moved to New Haven), Connecticut. 1701.
- Franklin's Academy (Penn)—Philadelphia, Pennsylvania. 1740.
- Princeton—Princeton, New Jersey. 1746.
- King's (Columbia)—New York, New York. 1754.
- Rhode Island (Brown)—Providence, Rhode Island. 1764.
- Queen's (Rutgers)—New Brunswick, New Jersey. 1766.
- Dartmouth—Hanover, New Hampshire. 1769.

A college was established in New England within the first decade of the Puritan Great Migration. This is indicative to some extent of their attitude toward learning. From the beginning, the religious impetus for settlement meant that New England had a significant number of educated immigrants. By the mid-1640s this included about 130 college-educated men, primarily from Cambridge, but it also included an educated middle class. This was reflective in part of their primarily East-Anglian origins and in part of the organized emigration led by ministers or gentry who recruited skilled individuals to accompany them.

Information about the attendees of colleges in New England is found in a comprehensive recent electronic publication, *Colonial Collegians* (see "Resources").

In New England, it was understood that it was beneficial to have an educated population. It was mandated that parents ensure their children's literacy, that towns of at least fifty families engage a school teacher, and that those with at least a hundred families offer a Latin school, but it was generally left up to localities to make arrangements, which often led to towns establishing the mechanism for setting up schools and hiring and paying teachers. The rest of America would ultimately benefit from this emphasis on public support for education when the New England model prevailed in the provisions for the surveying and distribution of public land by the Confederation after the Revolution, in which a section of land in every township was set aside to fund education.

The educational focus in New England was rarely without a theological component. The pulpit was a major source of information on matters both theological and political. Since church attendance in the earliest colonial times was mandatory, this very much set the tone for learning. Children learned from a *primer*, which probably contained an alphabet, the Lord's Prayer, the Apostle's Creed, the Westminster catechism, and a list of the books of the Bible. We aren't really sure— children were as hard on their schoolbooks then as now and almost none survived, although tens of thousands of copies of the *New England Primer* were produced.

Adults read newspapers, sermons, poetry, and histories (usually written with the theological overtone of why God especially favored New England). Broadsides, pamphlets, and books often presented theological and political points of view (somewhat like a modern editorial page); these also were widely read and discussed.

Reading material was produced both in England and on the presses in New England. The first complete Bible in America was printed on the Harvard press in 1663. See Morison, *The Intellectual Life of Colonial New England*, for details on education and reading material.[16]

You will not find school records in the colonial period, other than for the colleges. What you may find is evidence of and information about schooling and education in other records, ranging from court records of noncompliance to town records related to collecting rates or maintaining facilities.

Literacy

The literacy level in the colonies varied. When we consider literacy, we may be overly simplistic in our viewpoint. Reading and writing were separate elements. Often, individuals—particularly women—could read quite competently but could not write or even sign their names. Proficiency was related both to how much education your ancestor received and to the reality of how often as an adult your ancestor actually had occasion to read, write, and sign his or her name. Within a single family, we often find wide variation based on ability, desire, and the need to perform other activities such as household and farm tasks. Additionally, there is the question of the language of literacy. Your ancestor may have been able to read and write quite competently in another tongue, such as German, but have been shaky in English.

The degree of literacy in particular times and localities has been measured primarily by two measures—the presence of books in probate inventories and the number of individuals signing by name instead of a mark in deeds, depositions, and wills. The latter measure points to literacy in colonial New England of at least 90% for men and at least 40% for women by the end of the Revolution. The other colonial regions had much lower numbers. In the South there appears a much stronger class difference. Slightly more than half of landowners signed their names, while in the overall population barely 40% did so, with women a significantly lower 25%. In the middle colonies, the figures were in between. Fischer's *Albion's Seed* (see "Resources") has figures and additional analysis.

Lockridge, in *Literacy in Colonial New England*,[17] points out errors in some earlier analyses that indicated extremely high literacy in the earliest period and instead concludes there was a steady growth for men from roughly 60% to roughly 85% in the 1770s. After adjustments, he concluded that literacy outside of New England was 20 to 25% lower than in New England, did not show significant growth over time, and that this was not a result of German and Scotch-Irish immigration, but rather a lack of value placed on the expansion of education and literacy.

Not unsurprisingly, Lockridge found the rate lowest for laborers, followed by farmers, artisans, and merchants. More interesting, he noted that the rate of increase was greater in rural areas than in Boston, leading to equality in literacy by the Revolution. The literacy rate for women over time ran about half that for men.

The Calendar Change of 1752

Colonial research prior to 1752 requires an understanding of the calendar. The Julian calendar (established under Julius Caesar) was severely out of sync with nature's calendar by the 1500s. This created problems in establishing the date for Easter in the ecclesiastical calendar (described later in this chapter). Under Pope Gregory in 1582 a reform known as the Gregorian calendar was instituted. However, since this was a Catholic decree, many Protestant countries resisted the change. It was 170 years before England—which included the American colonies—finally made the change.[18] Several things happened with this switch.

Under the old (Julian) calendar, years ran from 25 March (Lady Day) to 24 March. The "first month" was March, and the "twelfth month" was February. The names of September, October, November, and December, based on their Latin roots, were derived from their positions as the seventh, eighth, ninth, and tenth months.

Under the new (Gregorian) calendar, New Year's Day became 1 January, rather than 25 March. For the first time in English history, the year changed on 1 January, and 31 December 1751 was followed by 1 January 1752. Interestingly, this makes 1751 the shortest year in modern history—it ran from 25 March to 31 December.

By 1752 the Julian calendar and the rotation of the earth were mismatched by eleven days. The decree that changed the beginning of the year also ordered the dropping of eleven days from the calendar. This correction was postponed until a slow period in September during which there were no major festivals and the English law court was not in session. Wednesday, 2 September 1752 was followed by Thursday, 14 September 1752. Thus, September 1752 was the shortest month in modern history with only nineteen days.

Publicity before the change instructed that contracts depending on elapsed time, such as mortgages and periods of servitude, would be governed by the time period (and therefore were to adjust the completion date). The general interpretation was that this also applied to birthdays. The emphasis was on age, not an immutable birth date. In other words, people who were 50 years and one day old on 2 September 1752 (i.e., born 1 September 1702) considered themselves 50 years and 2 days old on 14 September 1752, so they "changed" their birth date to 12 September 1702, which would have been their birth date if the new calendar had been in effect when they were born.

As you may recall from lessons in school, George Washington was born on 11 February (under the old calendar), but when he was an adult, his birthday was considered to be 22 February (under the new calendar). It is perfectly valid for an ancestor whose life spans the calendar change to have two birth dates, both of them correct.

It was no secret that the English were out of step. Other countries, including Scotland in 1600, had already moved New Year's Day to 1 January. Many record keepers acknowledged this potential confusion by double-dating events between 1 January and 24 March, so we often see 1689/90 or 1701/2 in records—even on gravestones.

A few record keepers designated dates done under the Julian system (the one beginning on Lady Day) as Old Style and wrote an "OS" after the date and those following the Gregorian system as "NS" for New Style. It is safest to put OS or NS in your records only if it was in the original.

Date Formats

In the colonial period we are likely to encounter several other variations in recording dates.

- *Last (ult.)*, *next*, and *instant*—as in 10th September last, 1 June next, or 12th instant—appear frequently in newspapers, financial records such as mortgages, court records, and personal letters. Although the meaning is altered by context, it isn't as difficult as it seems. *Last* means previous; in "15th last" the day is given, but the month is lacking, so *last* means last month. You also frequently see its Latin abbreviation *ult.* Similarly, "31 July next" indicates the next occurrence of 31 July after the document. *Instant*—or its common abbreviation *inst.*—means "this," for this month or this year.

- *Regnal years.* In England and the American colonies, deeds often have dates such as "the 5th year of George II." This is called a *regnal date* because it refers to the reign of the monarch. In American records, the "real" date is usually given also, so you rarely have to convert, but if you do, use the detailed table in *Black's Law Dictionary* (see "Resources"). There is a summary table in "Chronology" at the back of this book. In the town records of Acworth, New Hampshire, the town meeting of 28 February 1775 is identified as "in the fifteenth year of his magesties reign." That is the last time an English regnal date was used in the town's records. No matter what our history books tell us, one can see the subtle declaration of Acworth's independence in the early spring of 1775.

• Many people refer to phrases such as "first month" as *Quaker dating*, but this is something of a misnomer, as the practice of giving the number rather than the name of a month was common and not limited to Quakers. Through 1751, the first month in England and colonial America was March; beginning in 1752 it was January (see the discussion of the calendar change earlier in the chapter).

• 7^{ber} means September, 8^{ber} means October, 9^{ber} means November, and 10^{ber} means December. This was the record keeper's shorthand, based on the name of the month, not its position, and applies both before and after the calendar change.

The Ecclesiastical Calendar

Baptisms, marriages, and burials in church records are occasionally stated in relationship to days or seasons of the church calendar.[19] The

The courts in the American colonies were English courts, although the names, levels, jurisdic-tions and types of cases heard were reflective of the needs of the colony. Note the regnal dating, in which the date is given in terms of the reign of the current monarch. The English word "gaol" (jail) was routinely misspelled as goal in the colonies.

church calendar contains two different types of events: fixed and moveable. Fixed events, which are assigned to a specific date in the secular calendar, include feast days and saint's days. Easter, from which other moveable dates are determined, is calculated based on the weekly cycle, the solar cycle, the lunar cycle, and the secular calendar. While we may think of Easter as a single day, it is a season in the church calendar (as are Advent, Christmas, Epiphany, and Trinity), hence we may see dates such as the "second Wednesday of Easter."

Even nonchurch events reference ecclesiastical dates. In England, the judicial and business year were related to the ecclesiastical calendar. The English Court sits in terms referred to by ecclesiastical names: Hilary term (a bishop whose feast day is in January), Easter term, Trinity term, and Michaelmas term. Many business events, such as payments of rents, taxes, and bequests in wills and the duration of contracts and leases, occurred on one of the four "quarter days," which were Lady Day (March 25), Midsummer Day (June 24), Michaelmas (September 29), and Christmas Day (December 25). In the American colonies, we see this custom continued, as lease payments and quitrents were often due at the Feast of St. Michael the Archangel (Michaelmas).

We should always retain the original version of a date in our own files, so there can be no misunderstanding in the future.[20] Square brackets [ ] have universal meaning as an addition by the editor (you). Thus, you can accurately retain the original and add your interpretations, as in 27 February 1712[/3] or 3rd day 3rd month [May] 1740.

Currency

In the colonies, money was English-based—pounds, shillings, and pence—but there was a serious shortage of real currency. Standards for exchange included pieces of eight and other Spanish coins, Indian wampum, tobacco, and beaver pelts. Payments were routinely made in useful goods. In records, you may find entries written as £4.5.6 or $4^l\ 5^s\ 6^d$ for 4 pounds 5 shillings and 6 pence (the "d" for pence comes from *denarius*, or the Roman penny). There were twenty shillings in a pound and twelve pence in a shilling.

By the late 1730s, the situation was nearing crisis in Massachusetts. The colony did not have enough assets to issue secured currency and inflation was a decided problem. It was even proposed that new bills be valued at a different rate, hence the terms Old Tenor (OT) and New Tenor (NT) that can be seen in some financial documents of the times. During 1739, a Boston merchant organized what became known as the Land Bank of 1740. The circulating specie would be underwritten by the mortgages of the subscribers.

The topic dominated newspapers and the discussions in the General Court, but support for the Land Bank was widespread, both geographically and socially. Parliament issued an act forbidding it, causing outrage in the colony. This issue is considered a foreshadowing of the taxation-without-representation issue that ignited the American Revolution.

As the need for circulating money—both coin and paper—became more critical, the response was on a colony-by-colony basis, each issuing its own secured currency. The value of each against the English pound—and against the currency of the other colonies—varied considerably. Paper currency was generally considered worth less than the equivalent in coinage. Counterfeiting was common, as was clipping metal from the edge of coins. Both offenses were harshly punished. In 1764, the crown banned the further printing of currency in the colonies.

To learn more about currency, relative exchange rates, and the costs of commodities, see the Colonial Williamsburg website and McCusker's *How Much Is That in Real Money?*[21]

Given Names

The names given to children varied greatly among the American colonies and even over time within a single colony. A number of studies have been done about the types and frequencies of names chosen for children in colonial America that can help you in your research.[22]

Notes

1. John Putnam Demos, *The Unredeemed Captive: A Family Story from Early America* (New York: Alfred A. Knopf, 1994); Evan Haefeli and Kevin Sweeney, *Captors and Captives: The 1704 French and Indian Raid on Deerfield* (Amherst: University of Massachusetts Press, 2003); Emma L. Coleman, *New England Captives Carried to Canada between 1677 and 1760, during the French and Indian Wars* (Portland, Maine.: Southworth Press, 1925); Isabel MacBeath Calder, *Colonial Captivities, Marches, and Journeys* (New York, The Macmillan Company, 1935).

2. Isabel MacBeath Calder, *The New Haven Colony* (New Haven: Yale University Press, 1934) and Isabel MacBeath Calder, *Letters of John Davenport, Puritan Divine* (New Haven: Yale University Press, 1937).

3. George Madison Bodge, *Soldiers in King Philip's War, Being a Critical Account of that War with a Concise History of the Indian Wars of New England from 1620–1677* (Leominster, Mass.: the author, 1896), 413–46.

4. Modern literary writers have suggested that this term is incorrect and should be Scots-Irish. However, the use of *Scotch* in this context was and is prevalent throughout England and Scotland. See *The Oxford English Dictionary*. In the time period in which our ancestors lived, the term was definitely Scotch-Irish.

5. See George Madison Bodge, *Soldiers in King Philip's War, Being a Critical Account of that War with a Concise History of the Indian Wars of New England from 1620–1677* (Leominster, Mass.: the author, 1896); Douglas Edward Leach, *Flintlock and Tomahawk: New England in King Philip's War* (New York: W. W. Norton and Company, 1958); and Eric B. Schultz and Michael Tougias, *King Philip's War: The History and Legacy of America's Forgotten Conflict* (Woodstock, Vt.: Countryman Press, 1999).

6. US Bureau of the Census, *Historical Statistics of the United States: Colonial Times to 1970, Bicentennial Edition* (Washington: US Government Printing Office, 1975), Part 2, section Z, "Colonial and Pre-Federal Statistics," 1168. Adjustments have been made for charting consistency. The government figures have an anomaly in that they indicate that the combined populations of Plymouth Colony and Massachusetts Bay Colony were greater in 1690 than was the merged population in 1700.

7. Suggested reading includes, in order of publication: Charles W. Upham, *Salem Witchcraft with an Account of Salem Village* and *A History of Opinions on Witchcraft and Kindred Subjects*, 2 vol. (Boston: Wiggin and Lunt, 1867); Paul Boyer and Stephen Nissenbaum, *Salem Possessed: The Social Origins of Witchcraft* (Cambridge, Mass., and London: Harvard

University Press, 1974); Paul Boyer and Stephen Nissenbaum, *Salem-Village Witchcraft: A Documentary Record of Local Conflict in Colonial New England* (Boston: Northeastern University Press, 1982); John Putnam Demos, *Entertaining Satan: Witchcraft and the Culture of Early New England* (Oxford: Oxford University Press, 1982); Carol J. Karlsen, *The Devil in the Shape of a Woman: Witchcraft in Colonial New England* (New York: W. W. Norton and Company, 1987); Bernard Rosenthal, *Salem Story: Reading the Witch Trials of 1692* (Cambridge: Cambridge University Press, 1993); Mary Beth Norton, *In the Devil's Snare: The Salem Witchcraft Crisis of 1692* (New York: Alfred A. Knopf, 2002).

8. For a full discussion of Quaker meetings in New England, see Arthur J. Worrall, *Quakers in the Colonial Northeast* (Hanover, N.H.: University Press of New England, 1980).

9. See Patricia Law Hatcher, "Shipbuilding in Early America," *Ancestry Magazine* 23(May/June 2005), 6–41; also, for ground transportation, see "Jingle Bells," *Ancestry Daily News*, 27 December 2004. For water transportation, see "Row, Row, Row Your Boat," *Ancestry Daily News*, 1 February 2005.

10. An example for Scottish immigrants is Stephen M. Millett, *The Scottish Settlement of America: The Seventeenth and Eighteenth Century* (Baltimore: Clearfield, 1996).

11. Those with colonial-era entries include: David Dobson, *Directory of Scots Banished to the American Plantations, 1650–1775* (Baltimore: Genealogical Publishing Company, 1983); *Directory of Scottish Settlers in North America, 1625–1825*, 7 vols. (Baltimore: Genealogical Publishing Company, 1984–93); *The Original Scots Colonists of Early America*, 3 vols. (Baltimore: Genealogical Publishing Company, 1989, 1998, 1999); *Scottish Emigration to Colonial America, 1607–1785* (Athens: University of Georgia Press, 1994); *Scottish Soldiers in Colonial America* (Baltimore: Genealogical Publishing Company, 1997); *Scots in New England, 1623–1873* (Baltimore: Genealogical Publishing Company, 2002).

12. Lorenzo Johnston Greene, *The Negro in Colonial New England* (New York: Atheneum, 1942); A. Leon Higginbotham Jr., *In the Matter of Race: Race and the American Legal Process: The Colonial Period.* (New York: Oxford University Press, 1978), has sections on Massachusetts, New York, Pennsylvania, Virginia, South Carolina, and Georgia.

13. E. N. Hartley, *Ironworks on the Saugus* (Norman, Oklahoma, and London: University of Oklahoma Press, 1957).

14. Published several times, the earliest was probably *New England Historical and Genealogical Register* 1(1847): 377–79.

15. To learn more about colonial newspapers, see Frank Luther Mott, *American Journalism: A History of Newspapers in the United States through 250 Years, 1690 to 1940* (New York: MacMillan, 1941); Clarence Saunders Brigham, *History and Bibliography of American Newspapers, 1690–1820*, 2 vol., alpha by state, and *Additions and Corrections* (Worcester, Mass.: American Antiquarian Society, 1947, 1961); David A. Copeland, *Colonial American Newspapers: Character and Content* (Newark: University of Delaware Press, 1997); Sidney Kobre, *The Development of the Colonial Newspaper* (Gloucester, Mass.: Peter Smith, 1960); and William David Sloan and Julie Hedgepeth Williams, *The Early American Press, 1690–1783* (Westport, Conn.: Greenwood Press, 1994).

16. Samuel Eliot Morison, *The Intellectual Life of Colonial New England* (New York: New York University Press, 1936).

17. Kenneth Lockridge, *Literacy in Colonial New England* (W. W. Norton and Company, 1974).

18. Additional detail can be found in Robert Carver Brooks, "The Eleven Lost Days," *The Maine Genealogist* 21 (August 1999): 99–110; Gordon L. Remington, "Quaker Preparation for the 1752 Calendar Change," *National Genealogical Society Quarterly* 87 (June 1999): 146–50, 303; Mark M. Smith, "Culture, Commerce, and Calendar Reform in Colonial America," *William and Mary Quarterly*, Third Series 55 (October 1998): 557–84; Kip Sperry, "Time to Take Note; The 1752 Calendar Change," and Jake Gehring "A Brief History of Time," *Ancestry*, 18 (2000): 29–33.

19. Additional detail can be found in Patricia Law Hatcher, "The Ecclesiastical Calendar" *Ancestry Daily News* 17 April 2003; available at the Learning Center at Ancestry.com.

20. Additional detail can be found in Patricia Law Hatcher, "Recording and Interpreting Dates," *Ancestry Daily News* 23 August 2000, 30 August 2000; available at the Learning Center at Ancestry.com.

21. Ed Crews, "How Much is That in Today's Money?" *Colonial Williamsburg Journal* (online) <www.history.org/Foundation/journal>. John J. McCusker, *How Much Is That in Real Money? A Historical Commodity Price Index for Use as a Deflator of Money Values in the Economy of the United States*, 2nd ed. (Worcester, Mass.: American Antiquarian Society, 2001); this edition has better estimates, based on newer studies. At the Economic History Services website, you can ask for a conversion for dollars or pounds to current dollars; <www.eh.net/hmit>. For a discussion of currency and how trade was conducted, see Patricia Law Hatcher, "The King Was in His Countinghouse," *Ancestry Daily News*, 1 March 2005; "Ride a Cock Horse to Banbury Cross," *Ancestry Daily News*, 29 April 2005; and "Debits and Credits," *Ancestry Daily News*, 19 May 2005; available at the Learning Center at Ancestry.com.

22. George R. Stewart, *American Given Names* (Oxford: Oxford University Press, 1979. "Historical Notes" 1−42, "Dictionary" 43−258, "Notes" 259−264); David Hackett Fischer, "Forenames and the Family in New England: An Exercise in Historical Onomastics" *Generations and Change—Genealogical Perspectives in Social History*, ed., Robert M. Taylor Jr. and Ralph J. Crandall (Mercer University Press, 1986), 215−241. John G. Hunt and Donald Lines Jacobus. "Brothers and Sisters of the Same Given Names," *The American Genealogist* 36 (July 1960):158–59; Donald Lines Jacobus, "Early Nomenclature," *Genealogy as Pastime and Profession*, 28−33, 2nd ed. (Baltimore: Genealogical Publishing Company, 1968); George E. McCracken, "Early Middle Names," *The American Genealogist* 54(1978):108; Christine Rose, *Nicknames: Past and Present*, 4th ed. (San Jose: the author, 2002); and Daniel Scott Smith, "Continuity and Discontinuity in Puritan Naming: Massachusetts, 1771," *William and Mary Quarterly*, Third Series, 51:67–91.

CHAPTER TWO

Finding Information on Your Colonial Ancestors

The basic strategy for solid genealogical research is the same whether you are working before or after the American Revolution. What you will find to be different in colonial research is that you will rely much more heavily on printed sources than in Federal-period research. Follow this research strategy:

1. Collect as much information as possible from the federal and Revolutionary periods on your ancestors, including information on all members of their family, and on their neighbors and associates. Don't try to push backward or change localities too quickly.

2. Compile information in one place. Create a *documented* genealogical summary (family groups) and a chronology.

3. Read the "Background" section of this book to understand the context within which records were created and your ancestors lived.

4. Create a family/surname-based resource survey of what has already been published.

5. As you review published material that seems to relate to your ancestry, validate *everything*. Verify all key statements of relationship in original records.

6. Create a comprehensive locality-based resource survey.

7. Work your way through the locality-based list, beginning with local histories, and then reviewing published abstracts and electronic sources.

8. Read histories about the time and locality to learn more about your ancestors and their lives.

9. Compile what you have found and share it.

You Don't Have to Start from Scratch

One of the nicest things about colonial research is that many others have gone before you. Compared to federal-period research, you are more likely to be able to take advantage of the efforts of others to point you in the right direction and to save you time. People have been researching both history and ancestry for a very long time. The New England Historic Genealogical Society was founded in 1845; the earliest members had great-grandparents—and even grandparents— who were adults in the colonial period. So how do you tap into this treasure trove?

Use the work of others as guides, but verify what you find.

Some early researchers published all-my-ancestors compilations that are still highly respected today. Examples would be the multiple volumes of Walter Goodwin Davis, as well as Ferris's *Dawes-Gates Ancestry*.[1]

Some colonial compilations, however, aren't much better than many of the grab-a-name matchings we find in print and on the Internet today. How do you know which ones are respected? Reviewing articles in present-day scholarly periodicals (see "Resources") that build on and/or correct early lineages will help you understand the benefits and drawbacks of the research of early genealogists.

You cannot judge these works solely by the documentation. Standards of documentation have become more thorough in recent times because of the diversity of our research. In the early days of genealogical publication, when many of the sources were fairly obvious for the time and place, such standards were not as necessary. You may, in fact, need to become familiar with in-text citations and very abbreviated source identifications. There should, however, be sufficient information to allow you to determine where to obtain the information.

Some of the information in nineteenth-century genealogies going back to the colonial period was obtained through correspondence. The letter writers (who are often unidentified) may have had personal knowledge, a family Bible, letters, or other resources that provided the information—now all lost to us. If you are fortunate, the papers of the compiler have been deposited in a manuscript collection at an archives or library, which you may be able to track down.

Genealogical Compilations

After completing the foundation work in steps 1 and 2 mentioned previously, it is time to search for compiled information that potentially applies to your ancestral family. Look for distribution patterns of the surname. Although a few families remained in one locality for decades, even centuries, migration was the norm. You should examine all of the broad-based and easily searched resources in the following list, plus others depending on the time, the place, and how much you already know about the family (see "Resources" for details on these references):

- The surname section of the Family History Library Catalog.

- The surname section of *PERSI* (*PERiodical Source Index*).

- Anderson's *Great Migration* series.

- Austin's *Genealogical Dictionary of Rhode Island*.

- Compendiums of genealogies published in scholarly periodicals. For New England these include Connecticut, Plymouth, and Rhode

HISTORY

OF

ASHBURNHAM

MASSACHUSETTS

FROM

THE GRANT OF DORCHESTER CANADA

TO

THE PRESENT TIME, 1734—1886

WITH A

GENEALOGICAL REGISTER

OF

ASHBURNHAM FAMILIES

By EZRA S. STEARNS,

Author of the History of Rindge, N. H.

"Whate'er strengthens our local attachments is favorable both
to individual and national character. Show me a man who cares
no more for one place than another, and I will show you in that
same person one who loves nothing but himself."

ASHBURNHAM, MASS.:

PUBLISHED BY THE TOWN.

1887.

*Many nineteenth-century publications included both the history of a town and the genealogies
of its early families.*

Island genealogies from the *New England Historical and Genealogical Register* and other publications.

- Copeley's *Index to Genealogies in New Hampshire Town Histories*.

- Hollick's *New Englanders of the 1600s*.

- Longver and Oesterlin's *Surname Guide to Massachusetts Town Histories*.

- *Mayflower Descendant*.

- *Mayflower Families through Five Generations* and *Mayflower Families in Progress*.

- Mevers's "Consolidated Index to the Provincial and State Papers of New Hampshire" online.

- *New England Historical and Genealogical Register*.

- Noyes, Libby, and Davis's *Genealogical Dictionary of Maine and New Hampshire*.

- Savage's *A Genealogical Dictionary of the First Settlers of New England*.

- Torrey's *New England Marriages Prior to 1700*. Use the CD-ROM version that lists the sources in which the information was located. Often they were family histories covering many later generations.

Local Histories

As you build a locality-based list for the place your ancestor lived, you will discover a wide variety of resources. A good place to begin is with local histories. In New England, many of these include compiled genealogies or family sketches. There are great advantages in studying an entire community. One is less likely to make simplistic assumptions than with ancestor-focused research. However, as with all compiled research, you will want to verify what is there.

New England historians and genealogists of the nineteenth and early twentieth century prepared many in-depth, even multivolume, studies of individual towns and their early residents. Some were published as books, some got only as far as typescripts, and yet others survive only in the compilers' handwritten manuscripts. These are immensely important works for those with early New England ancestry; many of them have been reprinted or appear online.

In Connecticut we have such items as Barbour's *Families of Early Hartford* (a compiled, handwritten manuscript based on town records, six church records, two histories, and various family genealogies), Bowen's *History of Woodstock*, Calder's historical study *The New Haven Colony*, Cothren's *History of Ancient Woodbury*, and Jacobus's *History and Genealogy of the Families of Old Fairfield*, as well as his methodical eight-volume periodical compilation *The Families of Ancient New Haven*.[2]

Examples for Massachusetts and Plymouth colonies include Bond's *Genealogies of the Families and Descendants of the Early Settlers of Watertown, Massachusetts*, Hoyt's *Old Families of Salisbury and Amesbury, Massachusetts*, Perley's *History of Salem, Massachusetts*, Lincoln's *History of Hingham, Massachusetts*, and Sprague's manuscript *Genealogies of the Families of Braintree, Massachusetts*,[3] while New Hampshire has such items as Stearns's *History of the Town of Rindge* and Hosier's *Kingston*.[4]

Some of these are entirely in a historical format and some are entirely compiled genealogy, but most are a combination of both. A few include extensive abstracts of early town records, especially vital records. Don't neglect the historical section in your rush to find your family names. For one thing, the indexes to the original volumes rarely included every name, although some reprint publications have added every-name indexes.

Modern scholarly studies of the dynamics of the founding and governance of early towns can help you understand more about the lives of your own early New England ancestors, even if there is not a specific study for their town. Examples of these are Thompson's *Watertown* and *Cambridge Cameos* and Powell's *Puritan Village*, which is a study of Sudbury, Massachusetts, and winner of the Pulitzer Prize for History.[5]

Periodicals

Genealogical periodicals contain a variety of content of value for colonial research: abstracts of source data, compiled genealogies, problem resolution, history, and culture. Editors recognize that a journal publication needs to appeal to as broad an audience as possible, and since seventeenth-century persons will have more living descendants than, say, nineteenth-century persons, editors favor colonial articles. For more than a century and a half, genealogical and historical societies have published periodicals. The "Resources" section provides more information on periodicals of interest.

The New England Historic Genealogical Society, founded in 1845, publishes the *New England Historical and Genealogical Register* (NEHGR). The New York Genealogical and Biographical Society, founded in 1869, publishes the *New York Genealogical and Biographical Record* (NYGBR), which includes some articles on New Englanders. The Essex Institute began publishing the *Historical Collections of the Essex Institute* (later the *Essex Institute Historical Collections*) with irregular editions in 1869, lamentably discontinuing publication in recent years.

The *William and Mary Quarterly* (W&MQ), published by the College of William and Mary and Colonial Williamsburg Foundation, began in 1892 and has articles of interest from all of the colonies. Some publications of historical societies are titled *Proceedings* and consist primarily of papers prepared for lectures presented to the membership.

Most state and local genealogical societies were formed in the twentieth century. Many are still in existence; others had brief, yet valuable, publishing tenures. In New England, almost all societies are at the state level. The Maine Genealogical Society publishes the *Maine Genealogist* (formerly the *Maine Seine*). The New Hampshire Society of Genealogists published the *New Hampshire Genealogical Record* from 1903–1910 and resumed publication in 1990, while the Essex Society of Genealogists publishes the *Essex Genealogist*. The Connecticut Society of Genealogists publishes the *Connecticut Nutmegger*, and the Rhode Island Genealogical Society publishes *Rhode Island Roots*.

In addition, a number of journals have been privately published. *The American Genealogist* (TAG) began in 1922 as the locally focused *New Haven Genealogist*, but has become more national in scope. A majority of its articles cover the colonial period throughout New England and beyond. *The Genealogist*, formerly privately published, is now sponsored by the American Society of Genealogists. *Putnam's Monthly Historical Magazine*, focusing on Salem, Massachusetts, was published under several titles in the late nineteenth century. The *Rhode Island Genealogical Register* is still privately published.

Publications by societies formed around ethic, religious, or other specialized interests are useful to researchers who share that background. These publications may have both source material and valuable articles about culture and history.

Although the publications of hereditary societies focus primarily on their members and society activities, they may contain articles of interest, particularly in providing historical background. For example, the *Mayflower Descendant*, published by the Massachusetts Society of Mayflower Descendants, is an important source of abstracts for Plymouth Colony.

The variety of content in periodicals obviously indicates a variety of uses, from education to record abstracts. Perhaps the key question is, what will I find in periodicals that I won't find elsewhere?

A practical answer is that some items simply aren't massive enough to be a book. If your ancestor's church was in existence for only twenty years and all they kept was a book of minutes, records from it aren't likely to fit comfortably into any of the typical books of abstracts. But they are perfect for publication in a local periodical. Those minutes may mention in passing a family relationship that is not documented anywhere else.

Another practical consideration is that of corrections or additions. You may be lucky enough to find a nice thick family genealogy published in the 1930s. At that time it was much more difficult to access a large number of records than it is today. Thus, the book may have carried the male surname back many generations, but identified the maiden names of few wives. If a researcher today identifies one of those wives, he or she certainly isn't going to republish the whole book, but might be thoughtful enough to prepare an article—complete with documentation—describing the find.

Additionally, that family genealogy may have contained an error here and there, such as misidentifying a European origin or swapping cousins of the same name. Again, it is most likely that you will find the correction of these errors published in a periodical, not a book.

Scholarly journals are those with a critical editor who requires a high standard for the material published. These standards include the use of original sources, documentation, high standards of evaluating evidence, and research beyond one's own ancestral line. This is particularly valuable in compiled genealogies and articles tackling knotty problems. For colonial New England research, examples of notable scholarly journals are *NEHGR*, *W&MQ*, *TAG*, the *Maine Genealogist*, and *The Genealogist*.

Finding What You Want in Periodicals

The Family History Library Catalog categorizes periodicals under the locality. Use the Place Search for the county (repeat later for town and for state). The Place Details page will display a list of topics. You are likely to find entries such as Genealogy-Periodicals and History-Periodicals, but browse the full list, as periodicals may appear under other categories, too.

PERSI (*PERiodical Source Index*) was developed by the Allen County Public Library (Fort Wayne, Indiana), which has the largest collection of genealogical and historical periodicals in the country. Originally published in book form in more than two dozen large volumes, it is now available electronically. In 2004, it became available online to individuals through Ancestry.com and to libraries through HeritageQuest.com. Earlier releases, beginning in 1999, have been published on CD-ROM by Ancestry (see "Resources").

PERSI has three major sections: surname, locality, and general subjects, each of which can be searched by keywords. Most people go straight for the surname search, but don't neglect the other categories. The locality catalog also has specified subject areas, such as Cemetery Records. Thus, you can search for all articles about Ipswich, Massachusetts (be prepared for lots of hits); for Church Records in Ipswich; or for articles about tax records in New England. You may be surprised to note that some of the references occur in periodicals from states other than the locality of interest.

It is important to know that *PERSI* indexes just the primary focus of an article. (It is untrue, as is often claimed, that it only indexes names in article titles.) This is especially critical for compiled genealogies and articles correcting errors in publications. Be prepared with a list of all potential collateral lines and check those also, as you may find the information on your ancestor in an article about your ancestor's brother-in-law.

When you find a periodical article that looks interesting, you can click on the name of the periodical to display a list of some major libraries that hold the periodical.

The *Genealogical Periodical Annual Index* (*GPAI*) began publication in 1963 and was discontinued with entries from 2000 (see "Resources"). It indexed all names (including queries) in a wide variety of genealogical publications. It is a pure index—giving only the page reference, not the article title—so if the name you seek is not uncommon, you may be faced with dozens or even hundreds of entries.

Several of the most valuable periodicals are now available in electronic versions. Some are online, while others are on CD-ROM. See "Resources" for more details. We will surely see additional periodicals becoming available electronically in the future. You can usually search all volumes at once for a name, which is much faster than pulling dozens and dozens of volumes from the shelf to check individual indexes. As a by-product of this, it is much more likely that you will check for collateral names as well, which may lead to a breakthrough or prevent an erroneous conclusion.

Microfilmed Material

More than six decades ago the Genealogical Society of Utah (GSU)—the family-history entity of The Church of Jesus Christ of Latter-day Saints (LDS)—began microfilming records that would help its members research their ancestral families. A copy of the microfilm became part of the Family History Library (FHL) collection. The microfilm is available to anyone for a nominal rental fee at Family History Centers (FHC) and FHC-designated libraries.

In general, the microfilming process started in the oldest areas of the country—the original thirteen colonies—in state archives, county courthouses, town halls, private archives, and libraries: wherever permission could be obtained. Thus, for colonial research, you are likely to find your area of interest well filmed, more so than what you may have experienced in, say, the Midwest. It is often true that for colonial research a trip to Salt Lake City is a more efficient use of your research time and money than a trip to the area where your ancestors lived.

You should be aware when using the LDS microfilm, however, that the microfilmers had a list of records considered important for genealogical research. The list has varied over time (and is more flexible for localities that have suffered record losses). Thus, there may be some volumes that we understand today to be very useful that were not filmed initially. When microfilmers followed their list very literally, volumes with labels such as "Miscellaneous," "Mortgages," "Inventories," "Town Records" (unless they clearly contained vital records), and so on might have been skipped.

Additionally, many state archives also filmed their holdings. For some states, there may be both a state and an LDS microfilm for certain record groups. You may be able to borrow or buy microfilm from the state.

On-Site Research

Effective on-site research at an archives or courthouse requires effective off-site research in advance. First, identify and use any published resources (as described previously). Second, identify and use any microfilms done by the LDS church and state archives (as described previously).

Many state archives serve as the custodian not only for colony and state records, but also for older records from the counties. If you have several days in an area, this can save much time and money traveling from courthouse to courthouse.

Valuable features of archives include special indexes and card catalogs that have been prepared by the staff over decades in order to save wear and tear on fragile older records. These may include indexes to vital records, court records, naturalizations, land entries, and various county- and state-level records.

Some of these indexes have been microfilmed and are available at the Family History Library and other repositories. Some have been published in book form. Some are available on the Internet.

For example, the several New Hampshire card file indexes to vital records have been microfilmed; the Barbour Collection for Connecticut has been microfilmed and has now been published in book form; and the index to York County, Maine, Court Records 1686–1760 is on the website for the Maine State Archives (see "Resources").

If you do travel to an ancestral area to do research, knowing what to expect can increase the potential for discoveries and reduce the potential for frustration. Prepare for your visit on the Internet using a search engine or Cyndi's List (see "Resources"). Almost all archives and some counties have websites with driving directions, hours of operation, days of closing, and information about parking and handicap access. Many archives are not open on Saturday, and some are closed on certain weekdays. They often have restricted hours, opening later and closing earlier than you would expect. Many close for the lunch hour. Courthouses and town halls have similarly limited hours.

Arriving at an archives can be a process rather than an event. Because you may access irreplaceable manuscript materials, registration is usually required and restrictions apply to what you can take in with you. Be prepared. Allow for the extra time and be pleasant, remembering that staff members are, after all, protecting the materials so that researchers like you will be able to use them in the future. Usually you must complete a form. Take a photo ID with you.

Usually you are issued a key to a locker in which to place all nonpermitted articles. Some lockers are quite small, so leave unnecessary items in the car. Assume you will only be allowed a minimum of items with you—pencil, paper, and a few research notes. You will probably not be allowed purses, briefcases, files, coats, or similar items. Usually you can bring a laptop computer, but since many archives are in facilities that are more than a century old, there may not be electrical outlets.

Cutbacks in state budgets have hit archives especially hard. There are fewer staff persons to help you. In some states, the attitude of the staff is incredibly friendly and helpful. In others it is not. In many, the staff is simply overloaded.

When you've determined what records you want to look at, you may be surprised to be directed to a box of microfilm. Often it is the same LDS microfilm that you could have rented at home. Some archives have a limited number of microfilm readers; almost all are very old. Follow any restrictions about how long you can use the reader.

Although you are visiting "the archives," you may discover that many of the records aren't readily accessible and may even be stored off-site. It can take anywhere from a few minutes to several days to retrieve the records you request.

Often, you cannot make copies of documents yourself. If there is a machine, it may not be coin-operated. You may be required to purchase a copy card. In many cases, you are on the honor system. At the end of your visit, you are expected to report the number of copies you have made and pay for them all at once, so remember to count pages as you are preparing to leave.

Manuscript Collections of Original Records

Use on-site research time to access records and resources that are not available in other ways. Frequently referenced papers at state archives—especially those for the original thirteen colonies—often have been microfilmed, by the institution, the LDS church, or both. On the other hand, holdings of university and church archives and historical societies usually have not been microfilmed. Explore their online catalogs to identify manuscript holdings you want to investigate. Unlike a traditional library catalog, you may find entries that include background information on the collection and a detailed list of contents.

To find a neighbor's diary, a store ledger, or other manuscript, check the National Union Catalog of Manuscript Collections, affectionately known as NUCMC (pronounced "nuck-muck"), which contains summary descriptions of archives' manuscript holdings reported to the

Library of Congress. From 1959 through 1992, NUCMC was published in book form. Each volume is indexed separately, but there is a cumulative *Index to Personal Names 1959–1984* and a less-widely available *Index to Subjects and Corporate Names in the National Union Catalog of Manuscript Collections 1959–1984*. Entries beginning with the 1986–87 volume can be searched at the Library of Congress website. All years can be searched through the library subscription service, ArchivesUSA (see "Resources").

For New England, check the recent *Guide to the Manuscript Collections of the New England Historic Genealogical Society* by Salls (see "Resources").

Hints for Reading Colonial Documents

When reading early American documents, it is wise to divest yourself of any preconception of what is right or proper. Sometimes interpreting the handwriting is only the first battle if your transcript doesn't make modern sense.

We forget that our ancestors lived in a truly aural world. Our forgetfulness is understandable. We obtain our glimpses into their lives through written documents, but chances are that our ancestors rarely communicated among themselves through the written word, given that many of them couldn't read or write. Those who could do so usually had little time or reason to. Thus, we have a skewed view of their lives. Be flexible, remember that our ancestors lived in an auditory world, and you'll be more likely to understand what is written.

Words have not always been pronounced as they are now. It is important to remember that up until the Revolutionary War, we were part of England. In fact, we were English. So guess what? Americans had English accents.

Even though we live in a world of global communication, we still may find it difficult to understand every word in one of the British comedies or mysteries on PBS. England today is not a country of one accent. It certainly wasn't during the colonial period. When you consider the additional accents of those from English-speaking parts of the British Isles or under English colonial rule, you begin to get a better picture of the difficulty in communication, even among those whose native tongue was English. Another layer of difficulty occurs in differing language patterns and idiomatic expressions.

As other ethnic groups came in and we lost our ties to England following the Revolution, we developed our own linguistic styles, but then, as now, they varied considerably from one region to another.

Language is constantly evolving. New words come into use. Existing words drop out of use or change meaning. Pronunciation varies over time and place. Spelling of words and names was not standardized until very recently. In colonial America, phonetics ruled. There was no one right way to spell a word and word division was casual. Spelling varied even by the same individual. Do not assume that when you see a document with many words that you consider misspelled that the writer was ill educated.

Remember that our modern English language has many letters that are pronounced more than one way. When reading old documents, we must be even more flexible, especially in the pronunciation of vowels, and pay attention to context. For example, "dafter" (daughter) was sometimes pronounced to rhyme with "after," as it was in *Pilgrim's Progress*. We see the same switch commonly in "draftsman" and "draughtsman."

We must use great care in interpreting the names of individuals. Too often we fault the scribe when an ancestral name is "misspelled," and blame it on the lack of familiarity, but that is unfair. Family and friends may spell your ancestor's name in a variety of ways. Don't be surprised if your ancestor occasionally seems to vary the form of his or her own name.

Be aware that you will encounter terms that either are no longer part of our spoken language or that mean something different now. Check *Webster's Collegiate Dictionary*—and read all of the definitions. The best resource for archaic terms is the *Oxford English Dictionary*. Lederer's *Colonial American English* provides a survey of colonial terminology (see "Resources").

Use great caution in interpreting statements of relationship. *Brother* or *sister* can refer to a brother or sister by blood, by marriage, or in the church. Likewise, *son* or *daughter* might mean a birth, step, or in-law relationship. *Cousin* was widely used to refer to a wide variety of relations by both blood and marriage. *In-law* could mean *step*. Occasionally *niece* and *nephew* were used like their Latin roots to indicate grandchildren. It was common for a man to refer in his will to "my now wife." This is simply a legal phrase and does not imply anything about whether or not he had a previous marriage. We also find terms that denote status and respect, such as Goodman and Goodwife, Mr. and Mrs.

In the colonial period, handwriting contained several cursive letter forms that we do not use today. Several styles of handwriting were used in the colonies before the American Revolution. The further back your research takes you, the more unfamiliar letter forms you are likely to encounter in both uppercase and lowercase letters.

The best way to learn to read unfamiliar letter forms is to read and transcribe every word of a document. When we can read "and," "the," "day," "of," and "year," we are much more likely to be able to read the important words accurately. Another trick is to try writing in a colonial hand. As you practice forming words using upside-down r's and backwards e's, you'll rapidly gain the skill to read them more accurately.

Another difficulty in reading colonial documents is the lack of readily apparent sentences. You cannot rely on seeing a period followed by a capitalized word, which in modern writing indicates the ending of one sentence and the beginning of another. Sentences were often separated by dashes or colons or strung together one after another with an "&."

Our modern eye is further confused by the tendency to capitalize words that we wouldn't. Many scribes randomly capitalized words, irrespective of whether they were a noun, a verb, or an adjective. Even more annoying is the tendency to lowercase proper names. Sometimes it seems that the choice was determined by whether or not the scribe liked the capital version of a particular letter.

Colonial documents such as wills and deeds have a bit of structure, but there doesn't seem to have been any overwhelming compulsion to punctuate consistently, and commas and apostrophes were apparently considered an unnecessary extravagance.

Wavy lines and dashes were often used in legal documents to fill in at the end of a line so that no one could squeeze a word in unbeknownst. Breaking words when the scribe got to the end of the line—no matter where he was in the word—was the alternate approach to preventing inserted words. Syllables were irrelevant.

Not all legal language encountered in colonial documents is obsolete, but it isn't necessarily part of our daily reading and writing. Three words found in wills—*Imprimis, Item, Viz*—often were written in abbreviated form such as "Imp." or "It." These can be even more difficult to recognize because they begin with letters we rarely find as capitals.

- *Imprimis* means "first" (the first item).

- Each bequest is usually an *Item*.

- *Viz* means "to-wit" or "specifically" and is usually followed by enumerating details such as the names of all the children.

Written colonial English was filled with letters and symbols that we no longer see in written text.

- The thorn looks like a y but is pronounced "th." Thus, "Ye Olde Curiosity Shoppe" is pronounced "*the* old curiosity shop." There is much argument about which is the better way to transcribe the thorn. Generally speaking, until you are very experienced in transcribing colonial documents, you may prefer to type it as a y.

- The per looks like a p, usually with an extra-tall upstroke, and could be used to replace par, per, pre, pir, por, or pur anywhere in a word. Words in which you are likely to encounter this are "pcell" (parcel), "coop" (cooper), "psent" (present), "pte" (part), and "pfect memory" (perfect memory). The best way to transcribe the per is to add the missing letters within square brackets: "in the p[re]sence of."

- The long s looks almost like an f, whether handwritten or typeset, but transcribe it as an s. It almost always occurs as the first letter of a double s.

- The ff stood for a capital F at the beginning of a word. Like the thorn, you may find it safest to type what you see (ff) until you are very experienced in transcriptions.

- &, which often looks more like @ or ∝ in handwriting, frequently substituted for "and." The Latin for "and" is "et." Thus, it isn't surprising that you will frequently see "&c" (et c[etera]). Transcribe that as written.

The section "Dictionaries, Handwriting, and Law" in "Resources" lists many sources to help you in reading and understanding colonial documents.

Notes

1. Walter Goodwin Davis, *Massachusetts and Maine Families in the Ancestry of Walter Goodwin Davis (1885–1966): a Reprinting, in Alphabetical Order by Surname, of the Sixteen Multi-Ancestor Compendia (Plus Thomas Haley of Winter Harbor and His Descendants)* (Baltimore: Genealogical Publishing Company, 1996); Mary Walton Ferris, *Dawes-Gates Ancestral Lines*, 2 vols. (Milwaukee and Chicago: privately printed, 1943).

2. Lucius B. Barbour, *Families of Early Hartford, Connecticut* (Baltimore: Genealogical Publishing Company, 1977, from a typescript done by the Connecticut Society of Genealogists of the manuscript copy); Clarence Winthrop Bowen, *The History of Woodstock, Connecticut*, 8 vols. (Norwood, Mass.: Plimpton Press, 1926–43); Isabel MacBeath Calder, *The New Haven Colony* (New Haven: Yale University Press, 1934); William Cothren, *History of Ancient Woodbury, Connecticut: from the First Indian Deed in 1659, including the Present Towns of Washington, Southbury, Bethlehem, Roxbury, and a Part of Oxford and Middlebury*, 3 vols. (Waterbury, Conn.: William R. Seeley, 1871–79); Donald Lines Jacobus, *The History and Genealogy of the Families of Old Fairfield.* (New Haven: Tuttle, Morehouse and Taylor, 1930–32); Donald Lines Jacobus, *Families of Ancient New Haven*, 8 vols. (published as a periodical that later became *The American Genealogist*; reprinted in 3 vols., Baltimore: Genealogical Publishing Company, 1974).

3. Henry Bond, *Genealogies of the Families and Descendants of the Early Settlers of Watertown, Massachusetts, including Waltham and Weston, to Which is Appended the Early History of the Town.* 2 vols. (Boston: Little, Brown, 1855; available on CD-ROM from New England Historic Genealogical Society); David W. Hoyt, *Old Families of Salisbury and Amesbury, Massachusetts, with Some Related Families of Newbury, Haverhill, Ipswich, and Hampton, and of York County, Maine*

(Providence: the author, 1897–1919; originally published in 13 parts, then three volumes with a supplement, reprinted as one volume); Sidney Perley, *History of Salem, Massachusetts*, 3 vols. (Salem: the author, 1924–28); Georgeß Lincoln, *History of the Town of Hingham, Massachusetts*, 3 vols. (Hingham: the town, 1893); Waldo Chamberlain Sprague, *Genealogies of the Families of Braintree, Massachusetts, 1640–1850, including the Modern Towns of Randolph and Holbrook and the City of Quincy* (manuscript microfilmed by the New England Historic Genealogical Society in 1983 in cooperation with the Quincy Historical Society); information available on CD-ROM from the Society.

4. Ezra S. Stearns, *History of the Town of Rindge, New Hampshire, from the Date of the Rowley Canada or Massachusetts Charter to the Present Time, 1736–1874* (Boston: George H. Ellis, 1875); Kathleen E. Hosier, *Kingston, New Hampshire: Early Families, Patriots and Soldiers* (Bowie, Md.: Heritage Books, 1993).

5. Roger Thompson, *Divided We Stand: Watertown, Massachusetts, 1630–1680* (Amherst: University of Massachusetts Press, 2001); Roger Thompson, *Cambridge Cameos: Stories of Life in Seventeenth-Century New England* (Boston: New England Historic Genealogical Society, 2005); Sumner Chilton Powell, *Puritan Village: The Formation of a New England Town* (Middletown, Conn. Wesleyan University Press, 1963; available at libraries subscribing to <www. netlibrary.com>).

CHAPTER THREE

Colonial Records

M any types of records were recorded in the same way and in the same place both before and after the Revolution, and hence colonial research in those records is conducted in pretty much the same way as it is conducted for the federal period. The purpose of this section is to alert you to potential differences; it does not repeat basic information about standard records.

Format and Organization

Records in New England do not divide themselves nicely into classifications when it comes to where they were recorded and where you might find abstracts, transcripts, and published versions of them. Yes, there are land records, but in the earliest years they were recorded at the town level, all jumbled in with other records. Later—except in Rhode Island—they were recorded at the county level. Yes, there is a series of volumes referred to as "Massachusetts Vital Records," but those vital records come not only from town records, but also from county court records, church records, cemetery records, and miscellaneous records.

Fortunately, excellent finding aids exist for New England. The major repositories have online catalogs. The Genealogical Society of Utah did extensive microfilming in New England, so the Family History Library Catalog, organized by subject within locality, helps you work through at least part of this maze. More and more of the important colonial works are becoming available electronically on CD-ROM or on websites as databases, text, or images.

The earliest records were often kept in a single book, which included land transactions, taxation, probates, vital records, appointments, and anything else the town was concerned with, recorded chronologically. Interestingly, the business transactions often include the authorization to buy a new book. Sometimes a book was used for two purposes by turning it upside-down and beginning the second book from the back (which is always disconcerting to find on microfilm).

It is also not at all uncommon to find that at some point an attempt was made to group similar types of records together. This was not necessarily done by buying a new book, but by starting the new record set at a point in the midst of the blank pages later in the book. Although this probably seemed like a good idea at the time, the various sections didn't fill up at the same rate, so blank pages in another section were used, leaving a book that is consistent neither by record type nor by chronology. Usually after the first couple of mixed-use books, books became dedicated to specific types of records.

There may be problems about the naming and numbering of books. For example, the records of Westerly, Rhode Island, begin with Book 1: Westerly Town Records, Land Evidences, and so forth (1661–1706/7). When separate series were begun for land evidences, town meeting records, and vital records, those series began with volume 2, but the separate series for town council records and probate records begin with volume 1. For clarity, be as specific and as complete as possible when citing the title and volume number of an early record book.

We also have the problem of page numbers. In the earliest colonial period, pages had folio numbering. Technically, there was a single page number that applied to both the front (recto, right) and back (verso, left) of a sheet. However, in the creation of some later indexes (even in the nineteenth century), they indexed the unnumbered *facing* page, rather than the verso, with the written page number.

As if that weren't confusing enough, later an additional series of numbers, one per page, was often added. And, as most of us know, on microfilm any and all page numbers often fade into the unreadable dark areas in the top corners. When citing double-numbered books, it is useful to give both the folio number and the page number.

Historians and genealogists have long been mining the value of these earliest of American records, so they have been heavily used. Thus, the originals are often in very poor condition—far worse than what we usually encounter in the nineteenth century. Many early records were preserved by encasing them in silk, which reduces their legibility somewhat.

Even in the eighteenth and nineteenth centuries various governmental bodies and private individuals, observing the degradation of the original records, saw the value in creating transcripts or abstracts of the records. You may find that once a later, more readable, copy was created, the earlier copy was tossed out.

The Essex County Court ordered in the 1850s that a copy be made of Essex County vital records. For many towns, both handwritten versions have been microfilmed. Some of the clerks, when they could not read the original clearly, examined other records for clarification, so the copies are, today, better than the original.

Access

Accessing early records requires adaptability and organization on the part of the researcher. A variety of formats and access points is typical. Spend some time learning what was recorded, where it was recorded, and about any changes that have been made. Determine if the records—or a portion of them—are in print or have indexes.

Because colonial records so old, you will encounter a situation that is uncommon with federal-period records. You may be able to access colonial records—or information from them—in a bewildering variety of ways. You will find many ways to access the information in the records, and you should probably consult more than one.

Especially for the first half of the colonial period, there are often published abstracts, indexes, and transcripts of early records. They may

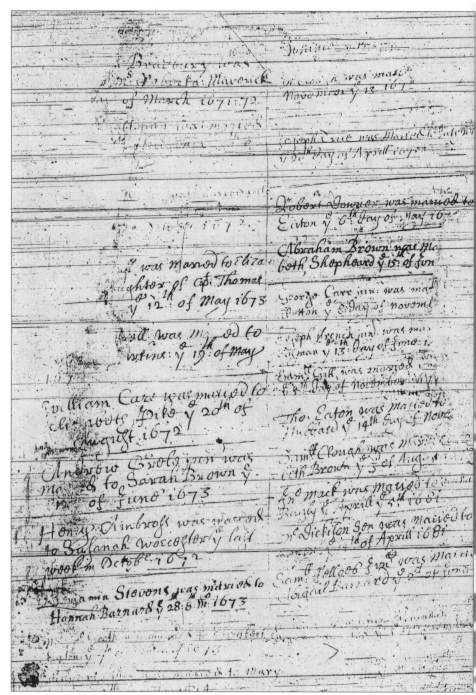

Early original records have been affected by centuries of use.

be in dedicated books, periodicals, town histories, collections of historical societies, or in publications sponsored by state or local governments.

Once you have identified the locality of interest, you should compile a complete bibliography of published works and investigate the contents of all of them. Don't assume that because a title says it is a history that it contains only history.

Don't quit until you have reviewed everything. Many records have appeared in different versions, in different combinations, in different arrangements, covering different time periods.

Just because something was published long ago doesn't mean that copies are difficult to find. Because these standard compilations and histories were done so long ago and are out of copyright, many have been reprinted. Furthermore, for the same reason, they were among the first to be converted to electronic text.

Many of these abstracts, indexes, and transcripts created by early researchers never made it past the handwritten or typescript stage and exist as single copies in manuscript collections or at archives. For example, in the 1910s Wyman abstracted the court files of Middlesex County, Massachusetts, for the years 1649 to 1675. His two volumes are in the manuscript collection at the New England Historic Genealogical Society. As is typical, these abstracts focus on the earliest period, but another two-volume set in the same institution, by Folsom and Rogers, provides an index to these court files that goes up through 1871. Until recently, examining these required a visit to Boston (which in and of itself is not a bad thing), but recently the society has added both of them to their online databases.

Town records and court records have often been combed for particular kinds of information. You may find abstracts concerning, in addition to vital records mentioned above, illegitimacy or ages in depositions, as in the publications by Sanborn.[1] You may also find books and articles that analyze particular elements such as Benton's book on warnings out throughout New England[2] or Thompson's *Sex in Middlesex*, which explores behavior and attitude.[3]

To avoid frustration and obtain maximum success when using early records, be flexible with your search and use the following guidelines:

- Don't just research your ancestor—research the jurisdictions and the records. Consult reference books, articles, and catalog notes.

- Consult reference materials to help you understand the arrangement and location of records.

- Seek out abstracts, transcripts, indexes, and analytical works that may help you get to the desired information more efficiently.

- Don't assume that records are to be found today in the locality of their origin; many have been transferred to centralized locations.

- Be actively aware of records newly available in a more accessible formats such as CD-ROM or online databases.

- Do not rely solely on the "title" of a record or a publication as the indicator of its contents. Read the catalog notes and introductions.

- Scan the entire volume to ensure that you understand what kinds of records are recorded therein and the arrangement thereof.

Often we must rely on later transcripts or copies sent to the county rather than the original. This clerk appears to have been bored.

- If the index seems to lead to the wrong page, examine a few pages earlier and later and try both page and folio numbering systems. A quick way to get back on track when you are having problems is to check in reverse—find the index entry for the name on the page that you are looking at, which will give you a clue about which direction to crank the microfilm.

Records of the Colonial Courts and Governments

The colonies were England—and yet they weren't. The first colonists inhabited a different landscape, with a different climate from what they had known for generations. There was no established infrastructure— no roads, no bridges or ferries, no businesses, no taverns, no courts, no schools, no teachers, no church buildings, no church hierarchy, often no minister, no graveyards, no docks, no houses, no barns, no fields, no farms, no garden plots, no fences. But the first colonists did have one thing that was not widespread in England—the ability to own land.

Each colony made legal, administrative, judicial, and ecclesiastical decisions based on what they had known in England, the differences in their new home, and the terms and objectives of the charter or proprietorship under which their residence was authorized. Thus, although the colonies had the same foundation and similar needs, the structures they developed were dissimilar, especially as they concerned land ownership.

In several of the colonies there were strong ties between church and state in the founding years, but only in New England did this connection direct the political structure. As discussed in the previous sections, the colonies of Massachusetts Bay, Plymouth, Connecticut, and New Haven were established with the goal of mandating a particular form of religion. There was little difference between the Puritan or Pilgrim leadership and the leadership of the colony. The structure, function, and goals of the courts—which initially were the main legislative body at the colony level—were very much in sync with the religious ideals of the leaders.

The division between the legislative, executive, and judicial branches that are the foundation of the federal period did not exist during the colonial period. The American colonies followed English law—both legislated and common law. The colonies operated under charters from the crown, which added another layer of control that dictated exactly how the legal system functioned. It also meant that systems differed under different charters, which reflected the agenda of the holder of the charter.

In general, in the earliest years, legislative, executive, and judicial functions were largely combined in one body. Anderson's "Colonial English Research" in the third edition of *The Source* deals more extensively with the peculiarities and problems of this early colonial period (see "Resources" for details). Once counties were established, most of the administrative (executive) and court (judicial) functions moved to the lower jurisdictional level.

The major early or colony-level publications are listed below (see "Resources" for details):

- **Massachusetts Bay Colony.** Early colony-level records are in Shurtleff's five-volume *Records of the Governor and Company of the Massachusetts Bay in New England, 1628–1686* and the three-volume *Records of the Court of Assistants of the Colony of the Massachusetts Bay, 1630–1692*. The nine-volume *Records and Files of the Quarterly Court, Essex County, Massachusetts, 1636–92* includes lengthy extracts of the documents filed with the cases. For Suffolk County see *Records of the Suffolk County Court 1671–1680*.

- **Plymouth Colony.** There are no early court records for Plymouth, but Konig's sixteen-volume *Plymouth Court Records, 1686–1859* covers the later period. Because Plymouth and the *Mayflower* are such a significant part of early American history, their records have been published and analyzed repeatedly, with Shurtleff and Pulsifer's twelve-volume *Records of the Colony of New Plymouth* providing the bulk of this material.

- **Maine.** Although a part of Massachusetts, York County (Maine's only county for most of the colonial period) maintained its own courts, whose records from 1653 to 1727 are published in the six-volume *Province and Court Records of Maine*.

- **Connecticut and New Haven colonies.** Trumbull's fifteen-volume *Public Records of the Colony of Connecticut, 1636–1776* and Hoadly's *Records of the Colony and Plantation of New Haven, from 1638 to 1649* and *Records of the Colony or Jurisdiction of New Haven, from May 1653, to the Union* cover the colonial period.

- **New Hampshire.** The forty-volume set of the *New Hampshire Provincial and State Papers* includes legislative, governmental, and court papers; early town petitions, charters, and papers; Revolutionary War Rolls and Oaths of Allegiance; and early probate records. Each volume contains an every-name index, but you can now access Mevers's two-thousand-page consolidated index on the website of the New Hampshire Division of Archives and Records Management. See "Resources" for further information.

- **Rhode Island.** Because of Rhode Island's lack of strong central government, records are in a variety of places. Consult Arnold's

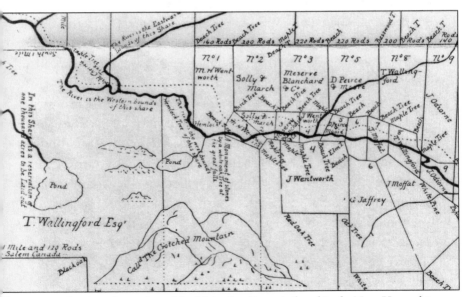

This section of a map of a portion of the Masonian Patent is found in the New Hampshire Provincial and State Papers.

The Records of the Proprietors of the Narragansett, Otherwise Called the Fones Record; the two-volume *Rhode Island Court Records: Records of the Court of Trials of the Colony of Providence Plantations, 1647–1670;* Fiske's *Gleanings from Newport Court Files, 1659–1783* and *Rhode Island General Court of Trials, 1671–1704,* and Towle's *Records of the Vice-Admiralty Court of Rhode Island, 1716–1752.*

Towns and Town Records

The lowest level of New England government was the town. In the earliest years, towns were often known by several names, including their Indian names. Thus, you may see references to Salem as Naumkeag, New Haven as Quinnipiac, New London as Pequot, Providence as Narragansett, and so on. We see this in the title of Banks's *History of York, Maine: Successively Known as Bristol (1632), Agamenticus (1641), Gorgeana (1642), and York (1652).*[4]

In the early colonial period there was basically a one-to-one match between towns and churches. Once the town was established, a number of practical matters would be addressed. This included electing the town leaders, filling town office, and voting on matters related to education and religion (including rates and taxation for funding, setting aside land for a church and cemetery, erecting and maintaining buildings, determining salaries, selecting personnel, and determining who sat in which pew).

The term *town records* (and *selectmen's records*) encompass many types of individual records. For example, the Family History Library Catalog has three entries under "Town records" for Methuen, Massachusetts. The catalog notes indicate that they include "selectmen's orders, records of valuation and taxation, and appointments . . . records of town meetings and reports . . . records of birth, marriage, death, and marriage intentions . . . warrants for town meetings, bonds, tax returns, reports, deeds, receipts, orders, records of earmarks, strays, persons warned out of town, fence divisions, accounts, bills against the town, estate records, military records, repair of highways, etc."

The Genealogical Society of Utah has filmed many New England town records, but only a few of them have been published, transcribed,

ı New England, many records are found at the town level, in town halls rather than county
ourthouses.

or abstracted—except for the vital records recorded in them. Published exceptions include such items as the Salem, Massachusetts, *Town Records, 1634–1691*, transcripts that were published originally as three volumes in the *Historical Collections of the Essex Institute*; and Swift and Cleveland's *Records of the Town of Tisbury, Massachusetts*. In Rhode Island, an early example is Snow's *Alphabetical Index of the Births, Marriages, and Death Records in Providence*, while the subtitle of Morgan, Bamberg, and Fiske's recent *More Early Town Records of Warwick, Rhode Island: "The Book with Clasps" and "General Records"* shows that early record books didn't necessarily have readily identifiable labels.[5]

The New England Historic Genealogical Society has helped make many sets of town and vital records available. As an example, for New Hampshire they published the Sanborns' two-volume *Vital Records of Hampton*, which includes entries from both church and town—often showing slight differences—and the Bow, New Hampshire, Town Records, 1727–1783, from a typescript in their manuscript collection, is on their website.[6]

For Dedham, Massachusetts, you would want to look at both Hanson's revised and expanded *Vital Records of Dedham, Massachusetts, 1635–1845*—which has entries from vital records, church records, newspapers, and diaries—and Lockridge's historical study, *A New England Town*.[7]

For New Hampshire we are lucky, in that there is a card index to the names appearing in the town records for the entire colonial period.[8]

Pay attention to the genealogy of any locality you are researching—and make certain that you look at all the resources available to you. Do not ignore publications—especially church records and histories—with the more modern place names in the titles. The records and history therein may cover time periods when the locality bore a different name. Also, people did not necessarily confine their activities to the locality in which they lived and may have left records in an adjoining jurisdiction.

As an example, the area that was originally Kittery, Maine, included what is today five different towns, some of which were not created until the 1800s. To begin a survey, you would look at Stackpole's *Old Kittery* and Her Families, Anderson and Thurston's Vital Records of Kittery, Frost and Anderson's Vital Records of Berwick, South Berwick, and North Berwick, and Anderson's Records of the First and Second Churches of Berwick, plus articles in the New England Historical and Genealogical Register by Dunkle and Ruocco for records of the First Church of Kittery and by Frost in the Maine Genealogist for records of the Second and Third Church of Kittery.[9]

The town government concerned itself not only with matters of administration, but also with matters that our modern viewpoint may find surprising. Towns were responsible for the welfare of their citizens. The people who "belonged" to the town were not necessarily all who inhabited the town. Thus, towns might "warn out" persons (quite often a family) who did not come from the town and whom they felt might turn out to be a drain on the social support system. This did not mean that the people necessarily had to leave, but it put everyone on notice that the town would not be responsible for their welfare. Sometimes an inhabitant of the town came forward to claim responsibility for an individual or family who had been warned out.

The eighteenth century showed a strong trend away from a church-state government, partly because of the existence of colonies—such as Rhode Island—that were not oligarchies, partly because of the growing number of immigrants who came for reasons other than religion, and partly because the subsequent generations had moved on in time, place, and interest from the church-led communities around Massachusetts Bay and the Connecticut River Valley. However, the congregational, community-based foundation was laid and continues to some extent into

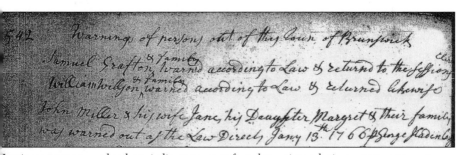

Warnings out were used to keep indigent persons from becoming a drain on town resources.

modern times. Today in New England, towns are still a basic governing unit. During national elections, camera crews focus on New England town meetings. Genealogists may find that old town records are still in the possession of the towns—occasionally in the personal possession of a town official, at his or her home.

Counties

Government by colony and town proved sufficient for the first decade of settlement, but by 1643, the population in Massachusetts Bay Colony had become extensive enough that routine matters could no longer be handled centrally, so the first county governments in New England were formed, establishing Suffolk, Essex, and Middlesex counties. In 1666, Connecticut formed counties—Fairfield, Hartford, New Haven, and New London. Plymouth Colony created three counties in 1685— Barnstable, Bristol, and Plymouth. Rhode Island formed two counties in 1703, but continued almost all recordkeeping at the town level. New Hampshire did not have functioning counties until the 1770s.

Very old records, especially at the county level, have often been transferred to somewhere other than what their description suggests. For example, Middlesex County court records are at the state archives, as are many other older records.

You may encounter the situation of obsolete or unexpected jurisdictions. Norfolk County in Massachusetts—or, as we more commonly say, "old" Norfolk County, since another county of that name was created in the federal period—is the one most likely to trip up genealogists. It covered the northern environs, so in addition to Salisbury and Haverhill in Massachusetts, researchers will find records of Dover/Strawberry Bank, Exeter, Hampton, and Portsmouth in present-day New Hampshire. Norfolk County was dissolved after 1679 when New Hampshire became a province. To complicate matters, however, deeds continued to be recorded as Norfolk deeds until 1714. (Note that there is no locality description for old Norfolk in the Family History Library Catalog, but there are references to it in the catalog under Essex County, Massachusetts; Dover, Strafford County, New Hampshire; and Rockingham County, New Hampshire.)

*arly record books often were used to record more than one type of record, as with this one,
hich included both vital events and deeds. Old Norfolk County, Massachusetts, which
cluded the towns of Salisbury and Haverhill in Massachusetts and Dover, Exeter, Hampton,
d Portsmouth in present-day New Hampshire was dissolved in 1679, but Norfold deeds
ere recorded later, and this book continued to be used into mid-eighteenth century by Essex
ounty, which gained custody of it.*

In western Massachusetts, the counties of Hampshire (created
1662) and Hampden (created 1812 from Hampshire) have an
unusual custody situation. The deeds of Hampshire prior to 1787 are
in Hampden. The Family History Library Catalog under Hampshire
County land records refers you, without explanation, to the Hampden
County microfilm. Citations should be perfectly clear, indicating that
you are citing Hampshire County deeds, from deed books in possession
of the Hampden County.

Naturalizations

Because the colonies were a part of England, those immigrants born
on British soil would not be naturalized. The colonies faced a quandary
when it came to immigrants who were not native born. Under English
law, only citizens could sell land, leave land to their descendants, serve
in the military, vote, and hold office. On this side of the Atlantic, the
realities of land settlement and ownership and the need for musters
to defend against threats prompted each colony to pass laws providing
for denizations—which conveyed to aliens a subset of the rights of
citizens—and for naturalizations. In 1740, Parliament passed an act

governing naturalizations, which was amended several times and rescinded in 1773.

It used to be difficult to determine if a colonial ancestor had been naturalized, but now Bockstruck's *Denizations and Naturalizations in the British Colonies* has gathered together the names in the surviving records into one place (see "Resources").

Vital Records

There are three groups most likely to have an interest in noting a vital event: the family, the church, and the government. Each group's interest in the vital event—and in creating records of the event—varies considerably based on time, place, and circumstance. Churches may have recorded baptisms rather than births, burials rather than deaths, and banns (Anglican) or intentions and accomplishments (Quaker) rather than the marriage itself. Family references would be found in private papers.

Even public records do not necessarily record the date of the event. Depending on the colony and time period, the record you find for a marriage may be an intention, a bond, a license, or a permission.

Although New England vital records were kept at the town level, this does not necessarily mean that an event recorded in a particular

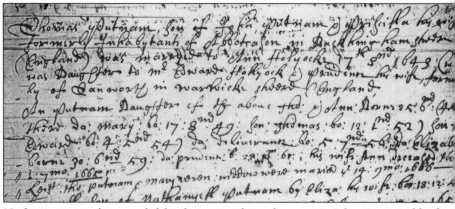

Vital events were often recorded family-group style, as they were in Salem (organized by first letter of last name), but rarely do they provide this much information. Notice the use of a col as punctuation.

town actually occurred in that town. Sometimes couples recorded their own births and those of their children, family-group style, when they moved to a new locality.

The vital records from both public records and church records have been published for a majority of New England towns. Some New England town histories included the early vital records. Be aware, however, that the earliest efforts often were expurgated, removing references to or records of fornication, illegitimacy, and other misconduct.

In addition to the Massachusetts *Vital Records through 1849* series (begun by the Essex Institute and continued by the New England Historic Genealogical Society), individuals have published volumes on individual towns in Massachusetts and elsewhere. A recent example is Stott's *Vital Records of Springfield, Mass. to 1850*, which includes information from all extant sources.[10]

Many of these publications include more than town vital records. In the *Vital Records through 1849* series, the codes on any non-town entry identify if a record came from a court record, a church record, a gravestone, or even private papers. Thus, you can consult a published series of "VRs," but the proper citation would also include "citing First Church" or "citing gravestone in Old Burying Yard." When possible— and for any crucial entry—you should try to examine the original.

In Connecticut, Lucius Barnes Barbour supervised the abstracting of town vital records. The Barbour Collection is at the Connecticut State Library, in two series. The entries were typed and bound in volumes, and arranged alphabetically by surname for each town. There is also a statewide slip (card) index, filed alphabetically by surname. For many years, using the Barbour Collection required a trip to New England. Then both the typescript volumes and the slip index were microfilmed. Recently White transcribed the typescript and published it in book form. Because both arrangements are alphabetical, any family-group arrangement is lost, although it can usually be deduced from the helpful page references. This does not, however, reveal whether any entries were made retroactively and did not actually occur in the town, something that may be suggested by analyzing the handwriting. Be aware, however, that in some cases the original is almost unreadable.

In New Hampshire, the various vital-records card indexes at the New Hampshire Division of Archives and Records Management has the interesting arrangement of being alphabetized by the first and third letter of the surname. It has been microfilmed and is available at the Family History Library, but seems to be alphabetically backwards on the microfilm. It is immensely useful, once you master the order, since each index covers the entire state (except for the town of Exeter).

Divorces were obtained by legislative petition in the colonial and early federal period and will be found in the legislative papers of each colony, most of which have been published.

Probate and Inheritance

Initially, in the founding years of a colony, matters concerning probates were handled centrally. As volume grew, more localized jurisdictions were established, but often probates were handled within the general court system. Only when that grew unwieldy were separate probate courts established.

Probate documents were recorded at the county level in Massachusetts, New Hampshire, and Maine; at the town level in Rhode Island; and at the probate-district level in Connecticut.

Published indexes or abstracts are often only for wills and do not include the many other aspects of probates, such as administrations, guardianships, inventories, bonds, and loose papers. You may have to dig more deeply for those.

- For Massachusetts, indexes are available for the counties of Essex,[11] Middlesex,[12] Plymouth,[13] Suffolk,[14] and Worcester.[15] The earliest records have been published for Bristol,[16] for Essex,[17] for Plymouth (in the *Mayflower Descendant*), and for Suffolk (in the *New England Historical and Genealogical Register*).

- New Hampshire's colonial probates are in the *Provincial and State Papers of New Hampshire State Papers*.[18]

- In spite of its general title, Manwaring's *Digest of the Early Connecticut Probate Records* covers Hartford District from 1635 to 1750, but includes records prior to its establishment.[19] In 1666, the probate districts of Fairfield, Hartford, New Haven, and New London—one per county—were established. In 1719, Guilford, Windham, and Woodbury were added. A dozen more districts were added before the end of the colonial period. See Melnyk's *Genealogist's Handbook for New England Research* for a table of the probate district for each town (see "Resources" for more details). There is also a state-wide index to loose probate papers at the Connecticut State Library, available on microfilm through the Family History Library.

In most cases, you will need to search the original records of the individual districts (usually there are volume-by-volume indexes).

*a localities where loose probate packets still survive, you may be able to find the original sig-
tures of family members in routine matters such as providing bonds or, as in this case, saying
ey didn't want to administer the estate. This document is from the very end of the colonial
riod; note that the handwriting style has changed to something that is easier for us to read.*

There is an index for Norwich District for most of the colonial period.[20] Sometimes early researchers, in seeking their own ancestry, generously abstracted all records for a locality and records group. Thus, to compile his Mead family history, Spencer P. Mead abstracted many church records in Fairfield County and the probate records for Stamford and Fairfield.[21]

• Rhode Island had the least-centralized probate system, recording everything at the town level. At the end of the nineteenth century a cumulative index was compiled by the city of Providence for its probate records.[22] For other towns, many early probates, recorded in town books, are abstracted in the *Rhode Island Genealogical Register*; a cumulative index to the deceased is in volume sixteen.

• In Maine, for complete coverage of probates, you need to check Sargent, Patterson, and Frost.[23]

Death, Cemeteries, and Gravestones

Death was an omnipresent part of colonial life. Epidemics of small pox, typhoid, and yellow fever recurred throughout the colonial period. Measles and diphtheria claimed the lives of many children. The deaths of women and children do not usually appear in probate records, but may be found on gravestones, in church burial records, occasionally in records of physicians, and mentioned in letters or diaries.

Colonial gravestones in New England are a rich resource. Not only do they provide vital dates of birth and death, the wording and

In New England, you can visit cemeteries that are more than three centuries old.

iconography of the stones tell us much about the beliefs of our New England ancestors. A walk through a New England graveyard is a walk back in time.

Gravestones and their carvers have been much studied, and many publications—with numerous illustrations—are available.[24] You may even be able to determine who carved your ancestor's gravestone. The excellent collection of Farber gravestone photographs can now be viewed on the Internet (don't just search for your family names—browse the collection for its rich images).[25]

New England had good native stone appropriate for carving gravestones, so very old stones can be found in almost every town. Gravestone markers are most likely to survive in clearly defined town cemeteries, church cemeteries, and inside church buildings. However, remodeling and expansion of church buildings has often caused the oldest stones to be moved or destroyed. In family cemeteries, graves were often marked merely by field stones, wooden graveboards, or wooden crosses.

Land

The earliest land records in New England are at the town level, but after the establishment of counties, they were kept at the county level—except in Rhode Island, where they continued to be entered at the town level.

The records of the first transfers of land, from town to individual, are usually in the town record books. There should be an accompanying plat, identifying the location of each lot. However, many of the plats were probably large separate sheets and did not remain with the books. If lot numbers were the identifiers for property, usually you can use a later map showing the lot numbers to identify your ancestor's lot. Town histories may have maps showing the lot numbers.

Microfilming of grants, patents, and deeds for the original colonies through about 1850 by the Genealogical Society of Utah was very thorough. A search can involve many rolls of microfilm. If you are planning a trip to the Family History Library in Salt Lake City, land-record research should be at the top of your priority list.

In New England, there has been less interest in publishing abstracts of colonial land records than in the South and the Mid-Atlantic, in part because some are at the town level.

- Land in Massachusetts was granted by the crown to the Plymouth Colony and the Massachusetts Bay Colony, who in turn "planted" towns. The proprietors of each town were responsible for distributing the land, usually by drawing lots, creating random initial settlement patterns. Initial grants are at the town level.

Bangs published Indian deeds for Plymouth Colony through 1691. Many Plymouth Colony deeds from the town records were published by George Bowman in the periodical *Mayflower Descendant*. Suffolk County deeds have been published in fourteen volumes; abstracts of the early Essex County deeds through 1678 were published recently by the Essex Society of Genealogists.[26]

In Massachusetts, Essex, Middlesex, and Worcester counties have two deed districts each; Berkshire and Bristol have three each, but they don't all have colonial deeds. Consult Melnyk's *Genealogist's Handbook* for which towns are in which districts and the custody information.

Two groups of early deeds—Ipswich Deeds and Old Norfolk County Deeds—are often overlooked for transactions in Essex County and in present-day New Hampshire and Maine. The town of Ipswich maintained its own extensive set of deeds, mortgages, and wills (but primarily deeds) from 1639–1695, independently of Essex County. Although dissolved in 1679, Old Norfolk recorded deeds until 1714.

- Early New Hampshire deeds were recorded in Ipswich or in Old Norfolk County. Initial transfers of land were done by town proprietors. Shortly before the Revolution, New Hampshire deeds began being recorded at the county level in the Office of the County Recorder.

- Prior to 1760, all of Maine was in York County; those deeds have been published in eighteen volumes through 1737.[27]

- In Connecticut, original grants were by the town proprietors. Deeds were recorded at the town level by the Town Clerk. There is an index to the deeds of the town of Hartford from 1639 into the nineteenth century.[28]

- Land transfers in Rhode Island are called "land evidences." Rhode Island followed the New England model of granting land to town proprietors, who then distributed the land to individuals. This distribution will be found in the Town Proprietors' Records, possibly in a separate volume. Subsequent transfers between individuals were also recorded at the town level.

  Early Rhode Island land evidences have been abstracted in the periodical *Rhode Island Genealogical Register*.

Maps

The earliest colonial maps are useful primarily for understanding how the rest of the world viewed the New World. You may be able to find more-detailed maps of the colonial period in local histories. Don't neglect to use property and tax maps of later periods. Several series of nineteenth-century maps have been republished in recent years and are identified in "Resources." Waterways, geographic features, and property lines usually did not change greatly after the colonial period (although the names may have changed), so you may be able to find the roads, churches, cemeteries, population centers, and individual homes in which you are interested, even though the map was made a century later. The exception to this is Boston, where much of the land that exists today was created by filling in the bay.

Lists

It is easy to overlook lists as a source because they are often part of a larger record group, rather than being a group unto themselves. Yet they are valuable tools for learning exactly where our ancestors were at a particular moment, who their neighbors and associates were, and a bit about their daily lives. Lists may help you discover that there were two men with the same name. Examples of lists you might use are as follows:

- **Immigration lists.** Other than port lists for London in 1634 and 1635 and arrival lists for Philadelphia of Germans, there are only scattered passenger lists or substitutes for passenger lists, most of which are in Coldham.[29] For New England through 1635, it is best to consult the compiled results for individuals in Anderson's *Great Migration* series (see "Resources").

- **Lists of officers and appointees of the town.** The main town officers in New England were called *selectmen*. A number of other appointments, usually chosen annually and rotating among the established citizens of the town were made. These can provide background, even if your ancestor is not named. Understanding why the town had to appoint fence viewers, a hog reeve, a pound keeper, or men to walk the bounds provides insight into the lives of your ancestors. Consult Lainhart's *New England Town Records* for descriptions of the responsibilities of each town office.

- **Lists of officers of the colony, county, or town.** Officials such as constables, gaol (jail) keepers, tithing men (tax collectors), and coroners were generally appointed each year. These are often found in court records. Magistrates sat at each court and ran it. At the beginning of any court session, there is usually a list of the magistrates present at that session.

- **Lists of freemen.** An inhabitant who could vote was called a *freeman*. In colonial New England, a freeman of the colony had to be a church member, although Connecticut gave the franchise for town elections to nonchurchmembers. The linking of land ownership to freemanship continued in Rhode Island and Connecticut longer than in the other New England colonies. Apprentices, servants, and women had no vote. Lists of existing and new freemen may be found in both town and colony records.

In the New England colonies, freemen did not vote on issues directly, but elected magistrates in whom was vested absolute authority.

- **Lists of representatives.** We have been electing representatives from lower jurisdictions to higher jurisdictions since colonial times. Occasionally, in addition to the list of representatives, you may find a list of voters—including for whom they voted.

- **Professional and business lists.** Certain professions and occupations, such as justices of the peace, notaries public, medical practitioners, lawyers, and sometimes clergy, had to be approved. Many types of professionals had to have a business license or permission to operate, usually on an annual basis. The same is true of certain types of businesses, such as ferries. Approvals such as these are often grouped together in town, county, or colony records.

- **Lists of inn keepers and tavern operators.** In the colonial period— and later in some locations—one couldn't just open a pub because it was a good business opportunity. Permission was required. Often need also had to be shown—on the part of the operator and of the potential customers. Preference was sometimes given to men who were disabled in a military conflict or widows. You may find that your ancestor signed a petition describing the need for a tavern in his neighborhood.

- **Lists of surveyors and road crews.** There was no Department of Public Works to build and maintain roads and bridges in early America. This duty fell on the citizens. In this context, *surveyor* sometimes can be interpreted to mean supervisor of a project. One of the immense values of these lists is that if the appointment is for a project in a particular area, the men named were usually from that same geographical area. This was a practical approach: the men who built or maintained a road or bridge would be the ones using it.

- **Jury lists.** Jurors were adults who had franchise (voting rights). Land ownership was often a prerequisite for voting and for serving on a jury. Grand juries and petit juries refer to the size of the jury (each of which heard certain types of cases), but there was no differentiation among who was appointed to which.

- **Lists of oaths of allegiance.** These are most commonly found if there had recently been a change of ruler, if there was potential of conflict over rule, or if the person taking the oath was changing the ruler to whom he was pledging allegiance. A related type of list, which is less common, is one of abjuration, in which the individual renounces allegiance to a ruler, either civil or religious.

- **Petitions.** People petitioned for a variety of reasons. They asked for bridges and roads, for changes in jurisdictional boundaries or the creation of new jurisdictions, for taverns, and for relief from a variety of taxes and duties. Often the original petition survives, with signatures—although the names may have been written down by a person organizing the petition, so compare the handwriting.

  Although they could not vote, women could, if appropriate, petition. In 1649, the women of Dorchester and Boston, Massachusetts, asked the General Court to remove restrictions placed on their midwife.[30]

- **Military lists.** Military preparedness and service prompted a variety of lists: militia lists (who was available), muster rolls (who showed up), absentee and sick lists (who didn't show up), pay lists, accounts, reimbursement for items lost in battles, officer appointments, and so on. These lists are found in county records, in colony and state records, and even in private hands.

  For example, the 1746 muster rolls of Capt. Ephraim Williams's Company and a list of men that went up to Otter Creek in 1747 are at the Massachusetts Historical Society in the papers of Israel Williams, who was the commander of the Hampshire County, Massachusetts, regiment during the French and Indian War.

- **Taxation lists.** These lists can yield invaluable information on individuals, their personal property, and their real property. But there are other types of assessments—usually specific to time and place—such as quitrent rolls or funds to pay the minister.[31] In New England, taxation was at the town level.

- **Membership lists.** Lists of church members are important, but can occasionally be difficult to interpret, since new members were often added to the lists without any indication of the date.

- **Lists of letters.** Newspapers often published lists of letters left at the post office (the early equivalent of "You've got mail!").

- **Pew lists.** It is a sign of the interrelationship between church and state in New England that pew lists are often found in town records rather than church records. People had assigned seats. Women, men, and children had separate sections. Seating was hierarchical, with wealthier, more prominent individuals seated at the front. However, special accommodation was often made for the elderly, placing them nearer the front so they could hear better or be nearer the stove (if there was one).

- **Livestock.** You will also find lists related to ordinary, everyday life, such as estray lists (livestock found wandering loose either taken home by the finder or placed in the local pound), marks and brands (to help identify the aforementioned wandering livestock), and bounties (to control the unwanted native animals).

How do you find these lists? Some, such as tax lists or oaths of allegiance, recorded in colony, state, county, or town records, have been extracted and published in separate volumes, but more often you will have to dig into the original record books to find them. Check the front

Wandering livestock that did damage to crops could be a serious problem. Estray notices are usually found in town records.

99

and the back for indexes. Often these volumes have index categories for specific types of lists.

Military Preparedness and Participation

For much of the colonial period, especially when there was an anticipated threat from the French and/or the Indians, local militia companies organized and trained regularly. In general, all able-bodied men were expected to participate, so although lists may have been kept for roll call, it was rarely necessary to retain such lists. The records you might find are more likely to be about an ancestor who didn't show up or who showed up improperly armed. During times of conflict, you are more likely to find records of the officers than of the rank and file.

The lists of officers and the full rosters that still survive were most often in colony-level records. Usually these are in print, often at least twice—once in the records of the colonial government (as mentioned earlier in this chapter) and again as direct off-prints or as transcriptions. Many libraries and databases that don't have the full colonial-records series will have the military subsets.

Published lists include the following:

- For Connecticut, there are two publications related to the Pequot War, one for Queen Anne's War and two for the French and Indian War.[32]

- For Massachusetts (which included Maine), the Society of Colonial Wars in the Commonwealth of Massachusetts has published six volumes of lists.[33]

- For New Hampshire, most of the lists are in the New Hampshire State Papers. Gilmore lists participants in the expedition to Cape Breton Island in King George's War.[34]

- For Plymouth Colony, lists are in Peirce.[35]

- For Rhode Island, you can consult three publications by Chapin, a portion of one by Smith, one by Peirce, and one by the Society of Colonial Wars in Rhode Island.[36]

Taxation

Tax records—which might be labeled valuations or assessments—may be created for the purpose of taxation of individuals (polls or tithes), taxation of real property (land), taxation of personal property, and dedicated purposes (paying a minister or funding a war). They can be valuable in several ways:

- They can tell you when your ancestor was alive, where he lived, and some indication of his age.

- They can tell you about the type and amount of land your ancestor owned.

- They can tell you about the livestock and other personal property your ancestor owned.

- They can provide a census of the community in which your ancestor lived.

- When tax rolls survive for a continuous run of years, they can help you determine changes in all of the above categories.

Taxation was generally at the town level in New England, so tax records will be found within the town records or in the office of the town assessor. There are rarely, however, consistent annual lists. Instead, occasional, stray lists may be found. For example, the New Milford tax list of 1756 was discovered in the papers of New Milford, Connecticut, town clerk John S. Addis.[37] An exception to town-level taxation is the 1760 to 1771 Massachusetts valuations, part of which have been transcribed by Pruitt and lists thirty-eight thousand persons with taxable property.[38]

Private Papers

Private papers—those documents created by individuals for their own use—are best explored without a specific research objective in mind. Instead, look at them with the general intent to get a glimpse of our ancestors' world. They may provide specific genealogical information about an ancestor. They may provide information about the life of a specific ancestor. Or they may provide information about the place and time in which an ancestor resided, without mentioning that ancestor.

Private papers include many types of records. There are diaries, letters, Bible records, business records, and professional records. Church papers are also private papers, but genealogists generally treat them as a research category of their own.

Journals and Diaries

Journals and diaries vary greatly in content. Some list daily events such as who visited whom or vital events. Others focus on activities of daily life.

The diaries of Thomas Minor and Manasseh Minor are important resources for events in Stonington, Connecticut, in the late seventeenth and early eighteenth centuries, and Joshua Hempstead's diary documents events in New London, Connecticut, in the mid-eighteenth century. The diary of Samuel Sewell Jr. of Brookline, Massachusetts, recorded events in the first part of the eighteenth century. The diary of Matthew Patten provides insight into life among the Scotch-Irish in the mid-eighteenth century in Bedford, New Hampshire.[39]

Some journals—more often those of the upper or educated classes—contain personal musings, political comments, and theological discourses. Clearly, some of these were penned with the clear knowledge that they would be read by others. Some men wrote histories of their times, often based on their diaries.

John Winthrop's journal was intended to become a History of New England and has been published as such. *The Journal of John Winthrop, 1630–1649* by Dunn and Yeandle is the best version. William Bradford wrote *Of Plimouth Plantation, 1620–1647.*[40]

Many bibliographies listing published and unpublished diaries, letters, and manuscripts are at libraries. These include Arksey and Reed, *American Diaries*; Forbes, *New England Diaries*; Goodfriend, *The Published Diaries and Letters of American Women*; Havlice, *And So to Bed*; Hinding, *Women's History Sources*; and Matthews, *American Diaries in Manuscript.*

Letters and Correspondence

Finding correspondence can be tricky, since letters end up in the hands of the recipient. There are two categories in which we can get a more complete record from the writer's perspective.

The first category includes published letters of a famous person, in which the editor has sought out surviving letters in collections of the recipients in a variety of institutions. An example of this is Calder's *Letters of John Davenport*, which gives insight into the settlement of New Haven, Connecticut.[41]

The second category is unfamiliar to researchers who have not worked in the colonial era. Many persons—particularly business, governmental, and professional men—kept what is called a "letter book" into which they or their clerk scribed a copy of each letter before it was sent. These were not confined to business matters, and often included purely personal correspondence and personal details in business letters.

Business Records

Business records are often found in archival collections. Both books and manuscripts are often catalogued under the locality, then a term such as "Business and Commerce." The archives may even have a separate finding aid for these records, as they are often used by social historians. You may also find extensive studies of colonial business records written by scholars and published by university presses.

If they are not too extensive, business records may be found in the journal of a genealogical or historical society. Some societies have published more extensive records as separate volumes.

There are many types of business records. Store records can give us much insight into the lives of residents. Most trade was on a credit basis, with the store keeping a detailed account of the purchases and then taking payment, usually after the harvest, in money or crops. Companies that bought, sold, and shipped crops and livestock may have useful records. Individuals or companies who sold land usually left extensive business records. Some ended up in state archives, others in libraries of colleges and universities.

The records of doctors, lawyers, and ministers are an important class of private papers.

The medical notebook of John Winthrop Jr., which is part of the Winthrop Papers at the Massachusetts Historical Society, has helped several genealogists persistent enough to decipher his notations solve knotty genealogical problems.

There is also a major category of what might be called "semiprivate papers." Notaries public and justices of the peace received official appointments, yet the functions they performed—scribing letters, business transactions, and documents such as wills and deeds—were for private individuals. Notaries and JPs had official status when documents such as acknowledgments were presented at court or recorded in, say, deed books. Many notaries and JPs kept private records of their actions, ranging from one-line abstracts of the action to full transcripts of everything they did.

In early New England we rely on the records of notaries Thomas Lechford (1638–41) and William Aspinwall (1644–51), both of which have been published.[42]

Finding Private Papers

Private papers can be very difficult to locate. Because they are private, many may still be in private hands. However, some families and businesses have understood that such records are better protected in archival institutions.

Be aware that this does not necessarily make them public property or even publicly available. Also, access requires time. It may take several hours or even days for records to be retrieved once you arrive at an archives. There may be restrictions concerning what you can do with the publication once you've found it. For example, you may be able to use the information, but not to publish an image or even a full transcript without permission. Some institutions are not fond of dealing with genealogists, having had bad experiences in the past. But if you plan ahead and are polite, patient, and persistent, and respect the rules and guidelines, you—and those researchers who follow you—will be able to use the records.

Explore the online catalogs of archives to identify manuscript holdings you want to investigate. Unlike a traditional library catalog, you may find entries that include background information on the collection and a detailed list of contents. Because private papers may end up in archives far removed from the events described therein, you should use an Internet search engine to determine if there are unexpected archives you would want to visit. You should also check National Union Catalog of Manuscript Collections (NUCMC) (see "Resources").

In library and archive catalogs, you must be flexible in searching. The subject categories used can vary widely. Items may be referenced at the community, county, or even state level.

If you are visiting Boston, check Salls's *Guide to the Manuscript Collections of the New England Historic Genealogical Society* (see "Resources").

Institutions acquire archival materials on an on-going basis. Thus, printed catalogs become outdated—as does your search of the online listing. How do you find out just what's new? Often a major genealogical or historical society that is associated with the collection publishes new manuscript acquisitions in its newsletter. Some list manuscript, book, and microform acquisitions in one merged list, but others have separate manuscript listings. Many have articles highlighting particular elements of the manuscript collection.

The papers of many important men have been published in multivolume sets. Often, at least a subset of these can be found on the Web, usually with images of interesting pages. Don't neglect these just because your ancestor wasn't important. As a government official, military officer, or business man, that important individual may have left papers that include a petition, muster roll, or account book with the name of your ancestor.

To find material from private papers published in periodicals, identify all the periodicals for the area of interest and investigate them. In the Locality section in *PERSI* (see "Resources"), letters are often listed as History or Biography and business records as History. Diaries may be classified as Church, History, Military, or Other.

Notes

1. Melinde Lutz Sanborn, *Ages from Court Records, 1636–1700: Essex, Middlesex, and Suffolk Counties, Massachusetts* (Baltimore: Genealogical Publishing Company, 2003) and *Lost Babes: Fornication Abstracts from Court Records, Essex County, Massachusetts, 1692 to 1745* (Derry, N.H.: the author, 1992).

2. Josiah Henry Benton, *Warning Out in New England, 1656–1817* (Boston: W. B. Clarke Co., 1911).

3. Roger Thompson, *Sex in Middlesex: Popular Mores in a Massachusetts County, 1649–1699* (Amherst, Mass.: University of Massachusetts Press, 1986).

4. Charles Edward Banks, *History of York, Maine: Successively Known as Bristol (1632), Agamenticus (1641), Gorgeana (1642), and York (1652)*, 2 vol. (Boston: Calkins Press, 1931–35).

5. William S. Swift and Jennie W. Cleveland, *Records of the Town of Tisbury, Massachusetts, Beginning June 29, 1669, and Ending May 16, 1864* (Boston: Wright and Potter Printing Co., 1903); Edwin M. Snow, et al., *Alphabetical Index of the Births, Marriages and Deaths Recorded in Providence*, 32 vols. (Providence: Sidney S. Rider, 1879; only *Vol. 1, 1636–1850* includes colonial entries); Marshall Morgan, Cherry Fletcher Bamberg, and Jane Fletcher Fiske, *More Early Town Records of Warwick, Rhode Island: "The Book with Clasps" and "General Records"* (Boston, Mass.: New England Historic Genealogical Society, 2001).

6. George Freeman Sanborn Jr. and Melinde Lutz Sanborn, *Vital Records of Hampton, New Hampshire, to the End of the Year 1900*, 2 vols. (Boston: New England Historic Genealogical Society, 1992); Bow [New Hampshire] Town Records, 1727–1783 (typescript at New England Historic Genealogical Society; available to NEHGS members at <www.NewEnglandAncestors.org>).

7. Robert Brand Hanson, *Vital Records of Dedham, Massachusetts, 1635–1845* (Camden, Me.: Picton Press, 1997). Kenneth Lockridge, *A New England Town: The First Hundred Years, Dedham, Massachusetts, 1636–1736* (New York: W. W. Norton and Company, 1970).

8. "Index to early town records, New Hampshire, early to 1850"; microfilmed on 111 rolls.

9. Everett S. Stackpole, *Old Kittery and Her Families* (Lewiston: Press of Lewiston Journal Co., 1903); Joseph Crook Anderson II and Lois Ware Thurston, *Vital Records of Kittery, Maine, Prior to 1892* (Camden, Me.: Picton Press, 1991); John Eldridge Frost and Joseph Crook Anderson II, *Vital Records of Berwick, South Berwick, and North Berwick, Maine* (Camden, Me.: Picton Press, 1993); Joseph

Crook Anderson II, *Records of the First and Second Churches of Berwick, Maine* (Camden, Me.: Picton Press, 1999); Robert J. Dunkle and Valerie Ruocco "Parish Records of the First Church and Society of Kittery, Maine, 1714–1791," *New England Historical and Genealogical Register* 151(1997): 39–58, 217–39, 353–70, 443–62; John Eldridge Frost, "Kittery, Maine, Third Parish Church Records," *Maine Genealogist* 21(1999): 125–32, 173–76; 22(2000): 25–30, 92–93, 139–40, 180–82; 23(2001):13–21; John Eldridge Frost, "Kittery, Maine, Second Parish Baptisms 1721–1831," *Maine Genealogist* 25(2003): 134–41, 180–90; 26(2004): 43–46, 83–93, 138–41, 183–89.

10. Clifford L. Stott, *Vital Records of Springfield, Mass. to 1850*, 4 vols. (Boston: New England Historic Genealogical Society, 2003; available on CD-ROM from New England Historic Genealogical Society).

11. Melinde Lutz Sanborn, *Essex County, Massachusetts, Probate Index, 1638–1840* (Boston: the author, 1987).

12. Samuel H. Folsom and William E. Rogers, "Index to the Probate Records of Middlesex County, Massachusetts, 1648–1871." 2-volume typescript at New England Historic Genealogical Society. Available to NEHGS members at <www.NewEnglandAncestors.org>.

13. Ralph Van Wood, *Plymouth County, Massachusetts Probate Index, 1686–1881* (Camden, Me. : Picton Press, 1988).

14. Elijah George, *Index to the Probate Records of the County of Suffolk, Massachusetts, from the Year 1636 to and including the Year 1893*, 3 vols. (Boston: Rockwell and Churchill, 1895).

15. George H. Harlow, *Index to the Probate Records of the County of Worcester, Massachusetts, from July 12, 1731, to January 1, 1920*, 5 vols. Worcester, Mass.: Oliver B. Wood, 1898–1920. Series A goes through 1881. Available to NEHGS members at <www.NewEnglandAncestors.org>.

16. H. L. Peter Rounds, *Abstracts of Bristol County, Massachusetts, Probate Records*, 2 vols. (Baltimore: Genealogical Publishing Company, 1987, 1988).

17. *Essex County, Massachusetts, Probate Records, 1635–1681*, 3 vols. (Salem: Essex Institute, 1916–20). Available on CD-ROM with Essex County Vital Records from Search and Research.

18. Albert Stillman Batchellor, Henry Harrison Metcalfe, and Otis G. Hammond, "Probate records from 1635–1771," *Provincial and State Papers of New Hampshire*, vols. 31–39 (Concord: State printer, 1867–1943).

19. Charles William Manwaring, *A Digest of the Early Connecticut Probate Records*, 3 vol. (Hartford: R. S. Peck and Company, 1904–6).

20. Jennie F. Tefft Gallup, "Abstracts of the First Probate Records of Norwich County, Connecticut, Volumes 1–3, 1748–1770" (typescript, by 1929). Available to NEHGS members at <www.NewEnglandAncestors.org>.

21. Spencer P. Mead, "Abstract of Probate Records for the District of Stamford, County of Fairfield, and State of Connecticut, 1729–1848" (typescript, 1941) and "Abstract of Probate Records of Fairfield, County of Fairfield, and State of Connecticut, 1704–1757" (typescript, 1934). Microfilm of copies at New York Genealogical and Biographical Society available at the FHL. The latter abstracts are available to NEHGS members at <www.NewEnglandAncestors. org>.

22. Edward Field, "Index to Providence, Rhode Island, Probate, 1646–1899" (Providence: The Providence Press, 1902). Available to NEHGS members at <www.NewEnglandAncestors.org>.

23. William M. Sargent, *Maine Wills, 1640–1760* (Portland: Brown Thurston, 1887). William D. Patterson, *The Probate Records of Lincoln County, Maine, 1760 to 1800* (Portland: Maine Genealogical Society, 1895). John Eldridge Frost, *Maine Probate Abstracts*, 2 vols. (Camden: Picton Press, 1991); abstracts only records not included in Sargent or Patterson; vol. 1 covers the colonial period.

24. *Markers*, publication of the Association for Gravestone Studies (278 Main Street, Greenfield, MA 01301; <www.GravestoneStudies.org>); Peter Benes, *The Masks of Orthodoxy: Folk Gravestone Carving in Plymouth County, Massachusetts, 1689–1805* (Amherst, Mass.: University of Massachusetts Press, 1977); Peter Benes, ed., *Puritan Gravestone Art*, 2 vols. (Boston: Boston University, 1976, 1978); Theodore Chase and Laurel K. Gabel, *Gravestone Chronicles: Some Eighteenth-Century New England Carvers and their Work* and *Gravestone Chronicles: More Eighteenth-Century New England Carvers and an Exploration of Gravestone Heraldica* (Boston: New England Historic Genealogical Society, 1990, 1997); Francis Y. Duval and Ivan B. Rigby, *Early American Gravestone Art in Photographs* (New York: Dover Publications, Inc., 1978); Harriet Merrifield Forbes, *Gravestones of Early New England and the Men Who Made Them, 1653–1800* (Boston: Houghton Mifflin, 1927); Diana Hume George and Malcolm A. Nelson, *Epitaph and Icon: A Field Guide to the Old Burying Grounds of Cape Cod, Martha's Vineyard, and Nantucket* (Orleans, Mass.: Parnassus Imprints, 1983); Allan I. Ludwig, *Graven Images: New England Stonecarving and Its Symbols, 1650–1815* (Middletown, Conn.: Wesleyan University Press, 1966); James A. Slater, *The Colonial Burying Grounds of Eastern Connecticut and the Men Who Made Them* (Hamden, Conn.: Archon Books, 1987).

25. Daniel Farber and Jessie Lie Farber, "Farber Gravestone Collection." <www.davidrumsey.com/farber>.

26. Essex Society of Genealogists, *Essex County Deeds, 1639–1678: Abstracts of Volumes 1–4 Copy Books, Essex County, Massachusetts* (Bowie, Md.: Heritage Books, 2003).

27. *York Deeds*, 18 vols. (Portland, Me.: John T. Hull, 1887–1910).

28. Levi Woodhouse, George S. Burnham, and Gordon Roberts *General Index to the Land Records of the Town of Hartford, from the Year 1639 to the Year 1839* (Hartford: Wiley, Waterman and Eaton, 1873). Available to NEHGS members at <www.NewEnglandAncestors.org>.

29. Peter Wilson Coldham, *The Complete Book of Emigrants, 1607–1660* (Baltimore: Genealogical Publishing Company, 1987); *The Complete Book of Emigrants, 1661–1699* (Baltimore: Genealogical Publishing Company, 1990); *The Complete Book of Emigrants, 1700–1750* (Baltimore: Genealogical Publishing Company, 1992); *The Complete Book of Emigrants, 1751–1776* (Baltimore: Genealogical Publishing Company, 1993); *The Complete Book of Emigrants in Bondage, 1614–1775* (Baltimore: Genealogical Publishing Company, 1988). These volumes are available on CD-ROM from Family Tree Maker. The subtitle of the main series—*A Comprehensive Listing Compiled from English Public Records of Those Who Took Ship to the Americas for Political, Religious, and Economic Reasons; of Those Who Were Deported for Vagrancy, Roguery, or Non-Conformity; and of Those Who Were Sold to Labour in the New Colonies*—defines a variety of reasons for emigration, and is an echo of the title of John Camden Hotten's earlier *The Original Lists of Persons of Quality, 1600–1700: Emigrants; Religious Exiles; Political Rebels; Serving Men Sold for a Term of Years; Apprentices; Children Stolen; Maidens Pressed; and Others Who Went from Great Britain to the American Plantations, 1600–1700, with their Ages, the Localities Where They Formerly Lived* (London, 1874).

30. Mary Beth Norton, "'The Ablest Midwife that Wee Know in the Land': Mistress Alice Tilly and the Women of Boston and Dorchester, 1649–50," *William and Mary Quarterly*, 3rd series, vol. 55 (January 1998): 105–34.

31. For more information see Patricia Law Hatcher, "The Taxman Cometh," *Ancestry Magazine* 21 (July/August 2003): 31–34.

32. James Shepard, *Connecticut Soldiers in the Pequot War of 1637* (Meriden: Journal Publishing Co., 1913); Donald Lines Jacobus, *List of Officials, Civil, Military and Ecclesiastical of Connecticut Colony from March 1636 through 11 October 1677, and of New Haven Colony throughout Its Separate Existence, also Soldiers in the Pequot War Who Then or Subsequently Resided within the Present Bounds of Connecticut* (New Haven: R. M. Hooker, 1935); Thomas Buckingham, *Roll and Journal of Connecticut Service in Queen Anne's War, 1710–1711* (New Haven: Acorn Club of Connecticut, 1916); Collections of the Connecticut Historical Society, vols. 9–10: *Rolls of Connecticut Men in the French and*

Indian War, 1755–1762; (Hartford: the society, 1903–05); and Frank DeWitte Andrews, *Connecticut Soldiers in the French and Indian War* (Vineland, N.J.: the author, 1923).

33. Carole Doreski, *Massachusetts Officers and Soldiers in the Seventeenth-Century Conflicts* (Boston: the society, 1982); Mary E. Donahue, *Massachusetts Officers and Soldiers, 1702–1722: Queen Anne's War to Dummer's War* (Boston: the society, 1980); Myron O. Stachiw, *Massachusetts Officers and Soldiers, 1723–1743: Dummer's War to the War of Jenkins Ear* (Boston: the society, 1980); Robert E. McKay, *Massachusetts Soldiers in the French and Indian Wars, 1744–1755* (Boston: the society, 1978); K. David Goss and David Zarowin, *Massachusetts Officers and Soldiers in the French and Indian War, 1755–56* (Boston: the society with New England Historic Genealogical Society, 1985); and Nancy S. Voye, *Massachusetts Officers in the French and Indian Wars, 1748–1762* (Boston: the society, 1975).

34. George C. Gilmore, *Roll of New Hampshire Men at Louisburg, Cape Breton, 1745* (Concord: Edward N. Pearson, 1896).

35. Ebenezer Weaver Peirce, *Civil, Military, and Professional Lists of Plymouth and Rhode Island Colonies, Comprising Colonial, County, and Town Officers, Clergymen, Physicians and Lawyers, with Extracts from Colonial Laws Defining their Duties 1621–1700* (Boston: the author, 1881).

36. Howard Millar Chapin, *A List of Rhode Island Soldiers and Sailors in King George's War, 1740–1748* (Providence: Rhode Island Historical Society, 1920), *Rhode Island Privateers in King George's War, 1739–1748* (Providence: Rhode Island Historical Society, 1926), and *Rhode Island in the Colonial Wars, A List of Rhode Island Soldiers and Sailors in the Old French and Indian Wars, 1755–1762* (Providence: Rhode Island Historical Society, 1918); Joseph Jenks Smith, *Civil and Military List of Rhode Island*, 2 vols. (Providence: Preston and Rounds, 1900–01); Peirce, *Civil, Military, and Professional Lists of Plymouth and Rhode Island Colonies*, . . . (see note 35); and *Nine Muster Rolls of Rhode Island Troops Enlisted during the Old French War* (Providence: Society of Colonial Wars in Rhode Island, 1915).

37. "Tax List of New Milford, Connecticut, 1756" from Thomas T. Sherman, "Old New Milford, Connecticut Records" (typescript, NEHGS). Available to NEHGS members at <www.NewEnglandAncestors.org>.

38. Pruitt, Bettye Hobbs. *The Massachusetts Tax Valuation List of 1771* (Boston: G. K. Hall, 1978; reprinted Camden, Me.: Picton Press, 1998).

39. Denison Miner and Hannah Miner, eds., *The Diary of Manasseh Minor, Stonington, Connecticut, 1696–1720* (n.p.: the editors, 1915); Sidney H. Minor and George D. Stanton Jr., eds., *The Diary of Thomas Minor, Stonington, Connecticut, 1653 to 1684* (New London: Day Publishing, 1899); "Diary

of Joshua Hempstead of New London, Connecticut Covering a Period of Forty-Seven Years, from September 1711 to November 1758," (typescript at the New Haven Colony Historical Society and the New London County Historical Society), available on microfilm at the FHL. The Sewell diary has been published in several versions, the most complete being Milton Halsey Thomas, ed., *The Diary of Samuel Sewell*, 2 vols. (New York: Farrar, Straus, and Giroux, 1973). *The Diary of Matthew Patten of Bedford, New Hampshire, from Seventeen Hundred Fifty-Four to Seventeen Hundred Eight-Eight* (Concord: Rumford Printing Company, 1903).

40. Richard S. Dunn and Laetitia Yeandle, ed. *The Journal of John Winthrop, 1630–1649* (Cambridge: Harvard University Press, 1996). It is available in both a full hard-bound version and an abridged paperback version. The abridged version excludes many mentions of individuals of interest to genealogists. William Bradford, *Of Plimouth Plantation, 1620–1647* (New York: Random House, 1981).

41. Isabel MacBeath Calder, *Letters of John Davenport, Puritan Divine* (New Haven: Yale University Press, 1937).

42. Thomas Lechford, *Note-book Kept by Thomas Lechford, Esq., Lawyer: in Boston, Massachusetts Bay, from June 27, 1638 to July 29, 1641* (Cambridge: John Wilson and Son, 1885); William Aspinwall, *A Volume Relating to the Early History of Boston Containing the Aspinwall Notarial Records from 1644 to 1651* (Boton: Municipal Printing Office, 1903; vol. 32 of Reports of the Record Commissioners of Boston).

CHAPTER FOUR

Expanding Your Research

C olonial settlement was very important to American history, so it has been written about many times. The interpretation and focus of historiography has varied considerably over time, so any book is reflective of the time period in which it was written. Additionally, historians bring personal viewpoints, ranging from cynical to idealistic, to their writings.

One of the best places to begin learning more about colonial life in general is your local library—preferably a branch library, not the main library. School children from elementary grades through high school are often required to learn about lifestyles of old, so you will find a substantial number of books with noncomplex descriptions of lifestyles, historical places, and events. Be aware, however, that books written for schoolchildren are usually simplistic and may have an agenda of presenting ideals and images that are not reflective of the broader range of events. In a library using the Dewey Decimal system, visit category 973.2 for general colonial information and the 97x category for the colony in which you are interested.

To get a balanced understanding of history and social history, read several books, preferably written during different time periods. The "Resources" section gives a sampling of titles to get you started. Once you've identified the library call number of a book, look for other titles with that call number. You will also find many websites with information about historical events or social conditions. The many interactive sites created by educational institutions specifically to help children understand history are most likely to be accurate.

Researchers interested in more in-depth learning will find many books published by university presses and articles in scholarly history journals. Do not limit your bibliographic survey to universities and journals in your state of interest. Most major university presses publish important studies covering the entire Atlantic region. *America: History and Life* is the annual index to the subjects of articles and book reviews in historical periodicals (see "Resources"). You'll find it in college libraries.

Historical Sites and Museums

There are many historical sites and museums focused on the colonial period. Their offerings range from old-fashioned display cases to movies to furnished homes to costumed reenactors. They offer a fun way to see

The Rebecca Nurse Homestead in Danvers, Massachusetts, is one of many colonial sites you can visit.

the items that would have been part of your ancestors' daily lives—and to do so in a way that your nongenealogically-inclined family members can enjoy also. You may have the opportunity to see an archaeological dig, taste colonial food, watch candles being made, or see a forge in operation.

A feature of special interest to genealogists is the gift shops of historical sites and museums, which usually have extensive offerings of books on history and on myriad aspects of everyday life.

Historic sites in New England with a colonial focus include the following (see "Resources" for contact information):

- Fairbanks House. Dedham, Massachusetts.
- Historic Deerfield. Deerfield, Massachusetts.
- Mayflower II. Plymouth, Massachusetts.
- Mystic Seaport. Mystic, Connecticut.
- Plimouth Plantation. Plymouth, Massachusetts.
- Rebecca Nurse Homestead. Danvers, Massachusetts.
- Saugus Iron Works. Lynn, Massachusetts.

Chronology

1607	Jamestown settled; first permanent settlement in English America.
1607	Sagadahoc (Kennebec River), Maine, settled; fails.
1620	Pilgrims land at Plymouth; first permanent settlement in New England.
1622	Monhegan, Maine, settled.
1623	Cape Ann, Massachusetts, settled under Roger Conant.
1623	Dover, New Hampshire, settled under Edward Hilton.
1623	Isles of Shoals, New Hampshire, settled.
1623	Rye, New Hampshire, settled.
1623	Saco, Maine, settled.
1623	Strawberry Bank (Portsmouth), New Hampshire, settled.
1623	York, Maine, settled.
1624	New Netherlands (New York) was settled by the Dutch at New Amsterdam (Manhattan).
1628	Naumkeag (Salem), Massachusetts, settled under John Endicott; the first under the Massachusetts Bay Charter.

1629	Charles I becomes king, increasing Puritan persecution in England.
1630	Winthrop fleet arrives in Boston, beginning the Great Migration, which lasted a decade.
1630	Charlestown, Massachusetts, settled by Puritans from England.
1630	Mattapah (Dorchester), Massachusetts, settled by Puritans from England.
1630	Medford, Massachusetts, settled by Puritans from England.
1630	Watertown, Massachusetts, settled by Puritans from England.
1631	Roxbury, Massachusetts, settled by Puritans from England.
1631	Newtown (Cambridge), Massachusetts, settled by Puritans from England.
1631	Saugus (Lynn), Massachusetts, settled by Puritans from England.
1632	Duxbury, Plymouth Colony, settled by Pilgrims.
1633	Aggawam (Ipswich), Massachusetts, settled.
1633	Marblehead, Massachusetts, settled.
1633	Scituate, Plymouth Colony, settled by Pilgrims.
1633	William Laud becomes Archbishop of Canterbury, increasing Puritan persecution in England to extreme levels and increasing migration.
1634	Catholic settlers, under Lord Baltimore's charter, arrive at St. Mary's in Maryland.
1635	Concord, Massachusetts, settled.
1635	Hingham, Plymouth Colony, settled by Pilgrims.
1635	Musketquid (Concord), Massachusetts, settled.
1635	Newbury, Massachusetts, settled.
1635	Wessaguscus (Weymouth), Massachusetts, settled.
1636	Harvard College founded in Cambridge, Massachusetts; first college in English America.
1636	Fort erected at Saybrook, Connecticut.

1636	Dedham, Massachusetts, settled.
1636	Hartford, Connecticut, settled by unhappy group from Newtown (Cambridge) under Rev. Thomas Hooker.
1636	Wethersfield, Connecticut, settled by unhappy group from Watertown.
1636	Windsor, Connecticut, settled by unhappy group from Dorchester.
1636	Narragansett (Providence), Rhode Island, settled by Rev. Roger Williams, fleeing Massachusetts.
1636	Springfield, Massachusetts, settled by unhappy group from Roxbury under William Pyncheon.
1636–37	Pequot War in Connecticut.
1638	First printing press in America, at Harvard College.
1638	Barnstable, Plymouth Colony, settled by Pilgrims.
1638	Exeter, New Hampshire, settled by unhappy group from Boston under Rev. John Wheelwright (Anne Hutchinson's brother-in-law).
1638	Hampton, New Hampshire, settled by group from Boston.
1638	Portsmouth, Rhode Island, settled by group from Boston under William Coddington and Anne Hutchinson.
1638	Quinnipiac (New Haven), Connecticut, settled by group from London under Rev. John Davenport and Theophilus Eaton determined not to stay in Massachusetts.
1638	Sandwich, Plymouth Colony, settled by Pilgrims.
1638	Swedish settlers come to Fort Christina in Delaware.
1639	Fundamental Agreement signed in Connecticut.
1639	Fundamental Agreement signed in New Haven.
1639	Colechester (Salisbury), Massachusetts, settled.
1639	Guilford, Connecticut (New Haven Colony), settled.
1639	Milford, Connecticut (New Haven Colony), settled by group from New Haven under Rev. Paul Prudden.
1639	Newport, Rhode Island, settled by unhappy group from Providence.

1639	Rowley, Massachusetts, settled.
1639	Sudbury, Massachusetts, settled.
1639	Taunton, Plymouth Colony, settled by Pilgrims.
1639	Mattacheeset (Yarmouth), Plymouth Colony, settled by Pilgrims.
1640	Mount Wollaston (Braintree), Massachusetts, settled.
1640	Marshfield, Plymouth Colony, settled by Pilgrims.
1640	Salisbury, Massachusetts, settled.
1640	Southhold, Long Island, settled by a group from New Haven Colony.
1641	Stamford, Connecticut (New Haven Colony), settled.
1642	Cape Ann (Gloucester), Massachusetts, settled.
1642	Warwick, Rhode Island, settled by unhappy group under Samuel Gorton.
1642	Woburn, Massachusetts, settled.
1643	Massachusetts forms counties.
1643	New England Confederation formed.
1643	Wenham, Massachusetts, settled.
1644	Branford, Connecticut (New Haven Colony), settled.
1644	Hull, Plymouth Colony, settled by Pilgrims.
1644	Reading, Massachusetts, settled.
1645	Rehoboth, Plymouth Colony, settled by Pilgrims.
1645	Manchester, Massachusetts, settled.
1646	Andover, Massachusetts, settled.
1646	New London, Connecticut, settled by a group from Gloucester, Massachusetts.
1646	Nawsett (Eastham), Plymouth Colony, settled by Pilgrims.
1647	Rhode Island receives royal charter, towns come together.
1649	Malden, Massachusetts, settled.
1649–60	Commonwealth in England ends need for Puritan migration to New England.
1650	Medfield, Massachusetts, settled.
1650	Natick, Massachusetts, settled.

1650	Scottish prisoners assigned to ironworks at Saugus (Lynn) and Braintree.
1651	Second group of Scottish prisoners arrive, sold as indentured servants.
1652	Dartmouth, Plymouth Colony, settled by Pilgrims.
1652	Kittery, Maine, organized.
1653	Kennebunkport, Maine, organized.
1653	Biddeford, Maine, organized.
1653	Wells, Maine, organized.
1653	Lancaster, Massachusetts, settled.
1655	Groton, Massachusetts, settled.
1656	Northampton, Massachusetts, settled by an unhappy group from Connecticut.
1659	Nantucket, Rhode Island (then New York), settled by group from Massachusetts, including Quakers.
1661	Hadley, Massachusetts, settled.
1662	New Haven Colony unites with Connecticut under a royal charter.
1663	Carolinas granted as proprietorships.
1664	New Amsterdam transferred to New England, becoming New York; settlements in New Jersey came under English governance and were granted as proprietorships.
1665	Newark, New Jersey, settled by a group from Branford, New Haven, Milford, and Guilford, Connecticut (New Haven Colony).
1666	Connecticut forms counties.
1669	Middleborough, Plymouth Colony, settled by Pilgrims.
1670	Deerfield, Massachusetts, settled.
1670	Hatfield, Massachusetts, settled.
1673	Northfield, Massachusetts, settled.
1675–76	King Philip's War devastates New England and Indians.
1679	New Hampshire becomes a separate province from Massachusetts.
1680	Old Norfolk County, Massachusetts, dissolved.

1681	First Quaker settlements in Pennsylvania.
1684	Massachusetts loses charter.
1685	Plymouth Colony forms counties.
1686	William Andros begins governing New England.
1686	Greenfield, Massachusetts, settled.
1689	William Andros kicked out of New England.
1689–97	King William's War, against the French. Colonists fight French and Indians.
1691	Massachusetts receives new royal charter.
1691	Plymouth Colony merges with Massachusetts.
1692	Salem witchcraft hysteria.
1702–13	Queen Ann's War, against the French and Spanish. Colonists fight French and Indians.
1703	Rhode Island forms counties.
1704	*Boston Newsletter* is America's first continuous newspaper.
1718	Significant numbers of Scotch-Irish begin arriving, settling Londonderry, New Hampshire, and elsewhere in Massachusetts and Maine.
1732	Oglethorpe receives charter for Georgia.
1744–48	King George's War, against French. Colonists fight French and Indians.
1747	Eastern border of Rhode Island established. Towns of Bristol, Cumberland, Little Compton, Tiverton, and Warren ceded by Massachusetts to Rhode Island.
1752	Calendar change. Ended use in England and colonies of Julian calendar in favor of Gregorian calendar.
1754–63	French and Indian War, against the French and Spanish. Colonists fight French and Indians.
1771–73	New Hampshire counties of Cheshire, Grafton, Hillsborough, Rockingham, and Strafford begin functioning (defined in 1769).

English Rulers of America

- Elizabeth I, 1558–1603
- James I, 1603–25
- Charles I, 1625–49
- The Commonwealth Period, Oliver Cromwell, 1653–58
- The Commonwealth Period, Richard Cromwell, 1658–59
- Charles II, 1660–85
- James II, 1685–89
- William and Mary, 1689–94
- William, 1694–1702
- Queen Anne, 1702–14
- King George I, 1714–27
- King George II, 1727–60
- King George III, 1760–American independence

Resources

Some of these sources will not be in genealogical collections, but are most likely to be found in college libraries. If the college near you does not have a book that you want, try interlibrary loan from your public library, as many colleges participate in the program. For background material, some preference has been given to books available in paperback that are traditionally used as supplemental reading in college courses.

Because of their enduring value, many of the older publications have been reprinted by one or more publishers. Where possible, the original publication data is given, to provide the reader with perspective. Reference works are cited with the most recent edition.

More and more of the important colonial works are becoming available electronically, on CD-ROM or on websites. Three websites for such electronic online versions are <www.Ancestry.com>, <www. HeritageQuest.com>, and <www.NewEnglandAncestors.org>. Many genealogical libraries have subscriptions to these services. You may also find electronic versions on the Internet or on CD-ROM of older books that no longer have copyright protection. Some books on history and social history are available through <www.netlibrary.com> at libraries that subscribe to that portion of the collection.

As you examine these resources or similar ones, use the notes and bibliographies therein to lead you to additional sources, especially those that may provide a slightly different viewpoint.

Resources, Reference, History, and Context

See also the specific colony sections that follow.

Akagi, Roy Hidemichi. *The Town Proprietors of the New England Colonies: A Study of Their Development, Organization, Activities, and Controversies, 1620–1770.* Philadelphia: University of Pennsylvania Press, 1924.

American Genealogical Biographical Index [AGBI], 206 volumes in the original series, 17 to date in the supplement. A project of the Godfrey Memorial Library in Middletown, Connecticut, this is an every-name index to the many volumes in their collection, which focus on New England. Available by subscription at <www.Ancestry.com>.

American Historical Association. *America: History and Life.* Annual publication of abstracts of articles and listings of book reviews from a variety of publications, including journals of state historical societies and dissertations.

Anderson, Robert Charles. *The Great Migration Begins—Immigrants to New England, 1620–1633.* 3 vols. Boston: New England Historic Genealogical Society, 1995. Some sketches available at Ancestry.com by subscription, and to NEHGS members at <www.NewEnglandAncestors.org>.

Anderson, Robert Charles, vols. 1–2 also George F. Sanborn, Jr., and Melinde Lutz Sanborn. *The Great Migration—Immigrants to New England, 1634–1635.* 4 vols. to date (through surnames beginning with L). Boston: New England Historic Genealogical Society, 1999–. Some sketches available to NEGHS members at <www.NewEnglandAncestors.org>.

Anderson, Robert Charles. "Colonial English Research," in Loretto Dennis Szucs and Sandra Hargreaves Luebking, eds., *The Source*, 3rd ed. Salt Lake City: Ancestry, 2006.

Anderson, Virginia DeJohn. *New England's Generation: The Great Migration and the Formation of Society and Culture in the Seventeenth Century*. Cambridge: Cambridge University Press, 1991.

Andrews, Charles M. *The Colonial Period of American History*. 4 vols. New Haven: Yale University Press, 1935+. Volume 1 won the Pulitzer Prize in History.

Andriot, Jay. *Township Atlas of the United States*. McLean, Va.: Documents Index, 1991. Shows present-day boundaries of townships and towns, but because many libraries have it, it is useful as a quick reference. Maps are by county, so for New England they are larger and easier to read than the ones in Melnyk.

Arksey, Laura; Nancy Pries; and Marcia Reed. *American Diaries: An Annotated Bibliography of Published American Diaries and Journals*. 2 vols. Detroit: Gale Research Company, 1983, 1987. Arranged chronologically, with name, subject, and geographic indexes; colonial diaries are at 1:3–82.

Bailyn, Bernard. *The New England Merchants in the Seventeenth Century*. Cambridge, Mass.: Harvard University Press, 1955.

Banks, Charles Edward [Banks manuscript]. 54 vols. at the Library of Congress, available on microfilm at many repositories. Includes information from both England and New England on many early New England settlers, although some of the pedigrees and potential pedigrees are erroneous due to the "name is the same" pitfall. His notes were published after his death by a noncritical compiler in Charles Edward Banks, Elijah Ellsworth Brownell, ed., *Topographical Dictionary of 2885 English Emigrants to New England, 1620–1650* (Baltimore: Southern Book Co., 1957).

Billington, Ray Allan. *Westward Expansion: A History of the American Frontier*, 5th ed. New York: Macmillan Company, 1982. The first eight chapters deal with the colonial experience.

Bockstruck, Lloyd deWitt. *Denizations and Naturalizations in the British Colonies*. Baltimore: Genealogical Publishing Co., 2004.

Boorstin, Daniel J. *The Americans: The Colonial Experience*. New York: Random House, 1958.

"Cemetery Transcriptions from the NEHGS Manuscript Collections." Available to NEHGS members at <www.NewEnglandAncestors. org>. The transcriptions come from a variety of sources.

Church of Jesus Christ of Latter-day Saints, The. Family History Library Catalog in FamilySearch <www.familysearch.org> A fast and easy-to-use CD-ROM version is available for purchase from the website at the extremely reasonable price of $5.

Clark, Charles E. *The Eastern Frontier: The Settlement of Northern New England, 1610–1763*. New York: Alfred A. Knopf, 1970.

Cooper, James F. *Tenacious of Their Liberties: The Congregationalists in Colonial Massachusetts*. New York: Oxford University Press, 1999. Available at libraries subscribing to <www.netlibrary.com>.

Crandall, Ralph J., ed. *Genealogical Research in New England*. Baltimore: Genealogical Publishing Company, 1984. Compilation of articles on each New England state, originally published in the *New England Historical and Genealogical Register*.

Cressy, David. *Coming Over: Migration and Communication between England and New England in the Seventeenth Century*. Cambridge, England: Cambridge University Press, 1987.

Cummings, Abbott Lowell. *The Framed Houses of Massachusetts Bay, 1625–1725*. Cambridge, Mass.: Harvard University Press, 1979.

Cyndi's List. <www.cyndislist.com>, created by Cyndi Howells, is the starting point for exploring what is available online and for accessing websites of courthouses, archives, and libraries.

Donahue, Brian. *The Great Meadow: Farmers and the Land in Colonial Concord*. New Haven: Yale University Press, 2004.

Earle, Alice Morse. *Child Life in Colonial Days*. New York: Macmillan, 1899.

"Early American Newspapers, 1690–1876," subscription service of Readex division of NewsBank, Inc. Currently available to members of the NEHGS and the New York Genealogical and Biographical Society.

Eichholz, Alice, ed. *Red Book: American State, County, and Town Sources*, 3rd ed. Salt Lake City: Ancestry, 2004. Organized by state, with each state covered by a local expert.

Eldridge, Larry D. *Women and Freedom in Early America.* New York: New York University Press, 1997. Available at libraries subscribing to <www.netlibrary.com>.

Fischer, David Hackett. *Albion's Seed: Four British Folkways in America.* Oxford: Oxford University Press, 1989. One of the folkways is "East Anglia to Massachusetts: The Exodus of the English Puritans, 1629–41."

Forbes, Harriette Merrifield. *New England Diaries, 1602–1800: A Descriptive Catalogue of Diaries, Orderly Books, and Sea Journals.* Topsfield, Mass.: the author, 1923.

Games, Alison. *Migration and the Origins of the English Atlantic World.* Cambridge: Harvard University Press, 1999.

Gaustad, Edwin S. *New Historical Atlas of Religions in America.* New York: Oxford University Press, 2001.

Gaustad, Edwin S. *The Great Awakening in New England.* New York: Harper and Row, 1957.

Gaustad, Edwin S., and Leigh E. Schmidt. *The Religious History of America*, 2nd ed. New York: HarperCollins, 2002.

Gold Bug, PO Box 588, Alamo, CA 94507; <www.goldbug.com>. A good source for old maps on paper and CD-ROM.

Goodfriend, Joyce D. *The Published Diaries and Letters of American Women.* Boston: G. K. Hall, 1987. Arranged chronologically, with name index; colonial items are at pages 1–13.

Greene, Lorenzo Johnston. *The Negro in Colonial New England.* New York: Atheneum, 1942.

Handybook for Genealogists, The, 10th ed. Logan, Utah: Everton Publishers, 2002.

Hatcher, Patricia Law. *Locating Your Roots: Discover Your Ancestors Using Land Records.* Cincinnati: Betterway, 2003.

Havlice, Patricia Pate. *And So to Bed: A Bibliography of Diaries Published in English.* Metuchen, N.J., and London: Scarecrow Press, 1987. Arranged chronologically, with detailed index; colonial American diaries are scattered throughout pages 13–51.

Hawke, David Freeman. *Every Day Life in Early America.* New York: Harper and Row, 1988.

Hinding, Andrea. *Women's History Sources: A Guide to Archives and Manuscript Collections in the United States*. 2 vols. New York: R. R. Bowker, 1979. Organized by location of repository.

Hollick, Martin E. *New Englanders of the 1600s: A Guide to Books and Articles Published 1980–2005* (Boston: New England Historic Genealogical Society, 2006).

Hone, E. Wade. *Land and Property Research in the United States*. Salt Lake City: Ancestry, 1997.

Hotten, John Camden. *The Original Lists of Persons of Quality, 1600–1700: Emigrants; Religious Exiles; Political Rebels; Serving Men Sold for a Term of Years; Apprentices; Children Stolen; Maidens Pressed; and Others Who Went from Great Britain to the American Plantations, 1600–1700, with their Ages, the Localities Where They Formerly Lived*. London: Chatto and Windus, 1874.

Kamensky, Jane. *Governing the Tongue: The Politics of Speech in Early New England*. New York: Oxford University Press, 1997. Available at libraries subscribing to <www.netlibrary.com>.

Krieger, Alex, and David Cobb. *Mapping Boston*. Cambridge: Massachusetts Institute of Technology, 1999.

Lainhart, Ann S. *Digging for Genealogical Treasure in New England Town Records*. Boston: New England Historic Genealogical Society, 1996.

Library of Congress. *National Union Catalog of Manuscript Collections*. Hamden, CT: 1959–1992. *Index to Personal Names in the National Union Catalog of Manuscript Collections 1959–1984*. 2 vols. Alexandria, Va.: Chadwyck-Healey, 1987. *Index to Subjects and Corporate Names in the National Union Catalog of Manuscript Collections 1959–1984*. 3 vols. Alexandria, Va.: Chadwyck-Healey, 1994. Search 1986–87 and later at <www.lcweb.loc.gov/coll/nucmc/rlinsearch.html> (select one of the RLG Union Catalog AMC File search forms). The full set of NUCMC is available at libraries with subscriptions to ArchivesUSA <archives.chadwyck.com>.

Main, Gloria L. *Peoples of a Spacious Land: Families and Cultures in Colonial New England*. Cambridge: Harvard University Press, 2001.

Matthews, William. *American Diaries in Manuscript, 1580–1954: A Descriptive Bibliography.* Athens, Ga.: University of Georgia Press, 1974. Arranged chronologically, with name index; colonial diaries are at pages 1–15.

Melnyk, Marcia D. *Genealogist's Handbook for New England Research,* 4th ed. Boston: New England Historic Genealogical Society, 1999.

Meyerink, Kory L., ed. *Printed Sources: A Guide to Published Genealogical Records.* Salt Lake City: Ancestry, 1996.

Morgan, Edward S. *The Puritan Family: Religion and Domestic Relations in Seventeenth-Century New England.* New York: Harper and Row, 1944.

Morgan, Edward S. *Visible Saints: The History of a Puritan Idea.* Ithaca, N.Y.: Cornell University Press, 1963.

Norton, Judith A. *New England Planters in the Maritime Provinces of Canada, 1759–1800; A Bibliography of Primary Sources.* Toronto: University of Toronto Press, 1993.

Norton, Mary Beth. *Founding Mothers and Fathers: Gendered Power and the Forming of American Society.* New York: Alfred A. Knopf, 1996. Covers 1620–70.

Osgood, Herbert L. *The American Colonies in the Seventeenth Century.* 3 vols. Gloucester, Mass.: Peter Smith, 1957. *The American Colonies in the Eighteenth Century.* 4 vols. Gloucester, Mass.: Peter Smith, 1958.

Paullin, Charles O. *Atlas of the Historical Geography of the United States,* Washington, D.C.: Carnegie Institution of Washington and American Geographical Society of New York, 1932.

Pope, Robert G. *The Half-Way Covenant: Church Membership in Puritan New England.* Princeton: Princeton University Press, 1969.

Price, Edward T. *Dividing the Land: Early American Beginnings of Our Private Property Mosaic.* Geography Research paper No. 238. Chicago: University of Chicago Press, 1995.

Reps, John W. *Town Planning in Frontier America.* Princeton: Princeton University Press, 1969.

RootsWeb. <www.rootsweb.com>, an organized, linked system of websites created by volunteers; now owned and hosted by Ancestry.com with free access.

Salls, Timothy. *Guide to the Manuscript Collections of the New England Historic Genealogical Society*. Boston: New England Historic Genealogical Society, 2002.

Sanborn, Melinde Lutz. *Supplement to Torrey's New England Marriages Prior to 1700*. 3 vols. Baltimore: Genealogical Publishing Company, 1991–2003.

Savage, James. *A Genealogical Dictionary of the First Settlers of New England*. 4 vols. Boston: Little, Brown, and Company, 1860–62. Available on CD-ROM from Family Tree Maker.

Sibley, John Langdon (vols. 1–3), and Clifford Kenyon Shipton (vols. 4–17). *Biographical Sketches of Those Who Attended Harvard College in the Classes 1751–1755 with Biographical and Other Notes*. 17 vols. Boston: Massachusetts Historical Society, 1965.

Smith, Juliana Szucs, *Ancestry Family Historian's Address Book*, 2nd ed. Salt Lake City: Ancestry, 2003.

Sperry, Kip. *New England Genealogical Research: A Guide to Sources*. Bowie, Md.: Heritage Books, 1988.

Sweet, William Warren. *Religion in Colonial America*. New York: Charles Scribner's Sons, 1951.

Szucs, Loretto Dennis, and Sandra Hargreaves Luebking, eds. *The Source*, 3rd ed. Salt Lake City: Ancestry, 2006.

Taylor, Dale. *Writer's Guide to Everyday Life in Colonial America, from 1607–1783*. Cincinnati: Writer's Digest Books, 1997.

Thompson, Roger. *Mobility and Migration: East Anglian Founders of New England, 1629–1640*. Amherst, Mass.: University of Massachusetts Press, 1994.

Thorndale, William, and William Dollarhide. *Map Guide to the US Federal Censuses, 1790–1920*. Baltimore: Genealogical Publishing Co., Inc., 1987. Does not cover colonial period, but because many libraries have it, the 1790 maps are useful as a quick reference.

Torrey, Clarence Almon. *New England Marriages Prior to 1700*. Baltimore: Genealogical Publishing Company, 1985. Available on a CD-ROM from NEHGS that also contains the reference entries from Torrey's manuscript at New England Historic Genealogical Society.

Tunis, Edwin. *Colonial Living.* New York: World Publishing Company, 1961.

Ulrich, Laurel Thatcher. *Good Wives: Image and Reality in the Lives of Women in Northern New England 1650–1750.* New York: Alfred A. Knopf, 1982.

US Bureau of the Census, *Historical Statistics of the United States: Colonial Times to 1970, Bicentennial Edition.* Washington: US Government Printing Office, 1975. Part 2, section Z, "Colonial and Pre-Federal Statistics."

UsGenWeb. <www.usgenweb.org>, an organized, linked system of websites created by volunteers.

Warren, Paula Stuart, and James W. Warren. *Your Guide to the Family History Library.* Cincinnati: Betterway Books, 2001.

Wehmann, Howard H.; revised by Benjamin L. DeWhitt. *A Guide to Pre-Federal Records in the National Archives.* Washington, D.C.: National Archives and Records Administration, 1989. Almost all of these records are from the Revolutionary period, rather than the colonial period.

Wilson, Lisa. *Ye Heart of a Man: The Domestic Life of Men in Colonial New England.* New Haven: Yale University Press, 1999. Available at libraries subscribing to <www.netlibrary.com>.

Winthrop, John. *History of New England from 1630 to 1649.* 2 vols. Boston: Phelps and Farnham, 1908.

Wright, Conrad Edick, project director, *Colonial Collegians.* CD-ROM. Boston: New England Historical and Genealogical Society, 2005.

Dictionaries, Handwriting, and Law

Black, Henry Campbell, *Black's Law Dictionary.* St. Paul: West Publishing Co.

Blackstone, William. *Commentaries on the Laws of England.* Chicago: University of Chicago Press, 1979.

Hatcher, Patricia Law. "Wordscape: Relativity," *Ancestry Daily News,* 31 May 2005; "Wordscape: Willing Words," *Ancestry Daily News,* 14 June 2005; "Wordscape: Wills and Special Cases," *Ancestry*

Daily News, 30 June 2005; "Wordscape: Other Probate Records," *Ancestry Daily News*, 12 July 2005; "Wordscape: Children in Court," *Ancestry Daily News*, 29 July 2005; "Wordscape: Apprenticeships and Indentures," *Ancestry Daily News*, 4 August 2005; "Wordscape: Court and Legal," *Ancestry Daily News*, 13 December 2005.

Kirkham, E. Kay. *The Handwriting of American Records for a Period of 300 Years.* Logan, Utah: Everton Publishers, 1973, 1981.

Lederer, Richard M. *Colonial American English, a Glossary.* Essex, Conn.: Verbatim Books, 1985.

Merriam-Webster's New Collegiate Dictionary. The classic, big, red dictionary you bought for school contains many of the words encountered in colonial research.

Oxford English Dictionary. Defines historical use of terms in great detail. Originally issued in 1933 in 13 volumes, it has been reprinted and updated (including a CD-ROM edition). The more recent two-volume *New Shorter Oxford English Dictionary* provides a less-cumbersome alternative.

Ross, Richard J. "The Legal Past of Early New England: Notes for the Study of Law, Legal Culture, and Intellectual History," *William and Mary Quarterly*, Third Series 50(1993): 28–41.

Ryskamp, George R. "Common-Law Concepts for the Genealogist: Real-Property Transactions," *National Genealogical Society Quarterly* 83(1996):165–81.

Salmon, Marylynn. *Women and the Law of Property in Early America.* Chapel Hill: University of North Carolina Press, 1986. Extremely useful for understanding how women's lives were restricted by the statute and common law that "protected" them.

Shammas, Carole; Marylynn Salmon; and Michel Dahlin. *Inheritance in America from Colonial Times to the Present.* New Brunswick: Rutgers University Press, 1987.

Sperry, Kip. *Abbreviations and Acronyms: A Guide for Family Historians,* 2nd ed. Salt Lake City: Ancestry, 2003.

———. *Reading Early American Handwriting.* Baltimore: Genealogical Publishing Co., 1998. Video: Kip Sperry, "Reading Early American Handwriting." Hurricane, Utah. The Studio, 2000.

Stryker-Rodda, Harriet. *Understanding Colonial Handwriting*. Baltimore: Genealogical Publishing Company, 1986.

Connecticut and New Haven

Until 1665, New Haven was an independent colony. In that year it was incorporated into the Colony of Connecticut.

Barbour, Lucius B. [Barbour Collection], Connecticut State Library. Typescript volumes of vital records organized by town and then by surname; statewide slip index alphabetized by name; available on microfilm (18 reels of typescript; 80 reels of card index). Typescript also published in 55 volumes: Lorraine Cook White. *The Barbour Collection of Connecticut Town Vital Records*. Baltimore: Genealogical Publishing Company, 1994–2002.

Collections of the Connecticut Historical Society, 31 vols. Hartford: the society, 1860–1932. Volumes 1–3 and 24 contain a variety of early documents. Volumes 4, 5, 11, 13, 15–19, and 21 contain papers of colonial governors. Volumes 9 and 10 are French and Indian War rolls. Volume 22 is the *Records of the Particular Court of Connecticut, 1639–1663*. Volumes 6 and 14 relate to Hartford.

Gallup, Jennie F. Tefft. "Abstracts of the First Probate Records of Norwich County, Connecticut, Volumes 1–3, 1748–1770" (typescript, by 1929). Available to NEHGS members at <www.NewEnglandAncestors.org>.

Genealogies of Connecticut Families from the New England Historical and Genealogical Register. 3 vols. Baltimore: Genealogical Publishing Company, 1983.

Hale, Charles R. [Hale Collection]. Typescript at the Connecticut State Library; available on 360 rolls of microfilm; mainly post-colonial records, indexing gravestone inscriptions and vital events in newspapers.

Hoadly, Charles J. *Records of the Colony and Plantation of New Haven, from 1638 to 1649: Transcribed and Edited in Accordance with a Resolution of the General Assembly of Connecticut*. Hartford: Case, Tiffany and

Company, 1857. *Records of the Colony or Jurisdiction of New Haven, from May 1653, to the Union: Together with the New Haven Code of 1656.* Hartford: Case, Lockwood and Company, 1858.

Long, John H., and Gordon Den Boer. *Connecticut, Maine, Massachusetts, Rhode Island Atlas of Historical County Boundaries.* New York: Simon and Shuster, 1994.

Main, Jackson Turner. *Society and Economy in Colonial Connecticut.* Princeton: Princeton University Press, 1985.

Manwaring, Charles William. *A Digest of the Early Connecticut Probate Records*, 3 vol. Hartford: R. S. Peck and Company, 1904–6.

Mead, Spencer P. "Abstract of Probate Records for the District of Stamford, County of Fairfield, and State of Connecticut, 1729–1848" (typescript, 1941). Microfilm of copies at New York Genealogical and Biographical Society available at the FHL.

———. "Abstract of Probate Records of Fairfield, County of Fairfield, and State of Connecticut, 1704–1757" (typescript, 1934). Microfilm of copies at New York Genealogical and Biographical Society available at the FHL. Available to NEHGS members at <www.NewEnglandAncestors.org>.

Scott, Kenneth, and Rosanne Conway. *Genealogical Data from Colonial New Haven Newspapers.* Baltimore: Genealogical Publishing Company, 1979.

Trumbull, J. Hammond. *The Public Records of the Colony of Connecticut, 1636–1776.* 15 vols. Hartford, Conn.: Case, Lockwood and Brainard, 1850–90.

Maine

Attwood, Stanley Bearce. *The Length and Breadth of Maine.* Orono: University of Maine at Orono Press, 1974.

Collections of the Maine Historical Society. 3 series, 22 vols. Portland: Maine Historical Society, 1831–1906. The petitions are especially of value to researchers.

Frost, John Eldridge. *Maine Probate Abstracts*, 2 vols. Camden, Me.: Picton Press, 1991. Abstracts only the records that are not included in Sargent or Patterson. Volume 1 covers the colonial period.

Haskell, John D. Jr. *Maine, a Bibliography of its History*. Boston: G. K. Hall, 1977.

Long, John H., and Gordon Den Boer. *Connecticut, Maine, Massachusetts, Rhode Island Atlas of Historical County Boundaries*. New York: Simon and Shuster, 1994.

Morris, Gerald E. *Maine Bicentennial Atlas*. Portland: Maine Historical Society, 1976.

Noyes, Sybil; Charles Thornton Libby; and Walter Goodwin Davis. *Genealogical Dictionary of Maine and New Hampshire*. 2 vols. Portland, Me.: Southworth Press, 1928–9. Available by subscription from Ancestry.com and on CD-ROM from Family Tree Maker.

Old Maps of [county] *Maine*, series by county, maps from latter half of nineteenth century. Fryeburg: Saco Valley Printing, 1980s.

Patterson, William D. *The Probate Records of Lincoln County, Maine, 1760 to 1800*. Portland: Maine Genealogical Society, 1895.

Pope, Charles Henry. *The Pioneers of Maine and New Hampshire, 1623 to 1660: a Descriptive List, Drawn from Records of the Colonies, Towns, Churches, Courts and Other Contemporary Sources*. Boston: the author, 1908.

Province and Court Records of Maine. 6 vols. Portland: Maine Historical Society, 1928–1975. Includes York County court records, 1653–1727.

Rutherford, Phillip R. *Dictionary of Maine Place-Names*. Freeport: Bond Wheelwright Company, 1970.

Sargent, William M. *Maine Wills, 1640–1760*. Portland, Me.: Brown Thurston, 1887.

Williamson, William D. *The History of the State of Maine from Its First Discovery, A.D. 1602, to the Separation, A.D. 1820 Inclusive*. Hallowell, Me.: Glazier, Masters and Company, 1832.

York Deeds. 18 vols. Portland, Me.: John T. Hull, 1887–1910. Prior to 1760, Maine was in York County; these deeds go through 1737.

Massachusetts

For Plymouth Colony, which merged with Massachusetts in 1691, see the following:

Aspinwall, William. *A Volume Relating to the Early History of Boston Containing the Aspinwall Notarial Records from 1644 to 1651.* Boston: Municipal Printing Office, 1903 (vol. 32 of Reports of the Record Commissioners of Boston).

Bremer, Francis J. *John Winthrop: America's Forgotten Founding Father.* New York: Oxford University Press, 2003.

Bremer, Francis J. *The Puritan Experiment: New England Society from Bradford to Edwards.* New York: St. Martin's Press, 1976.

Collections of the Massachusetts Historical Society. Seven series, begun in 1792, continuing through the early twentieth century. They include such items as the Winthrop Papers.

Corbin, Walter E., and Lottie Squier Corbin [Corbin Collection]. Manuscript collection at New England Historic Genealogical Society, 60 rolls of microfilm. Available on CD-ROM (edited by Robert J. Dunkle) from New England Historic Genealogical Society, currently being released.

Davis, Charlotte Pease. *Directory of Massachusetts Place Names.* Lexington: Bay State News, 1987.

Denis, Michael J. *Massachusetts Towns and Counties.* Oakland, Me.: Danbury House Books, 1984.

Dow, George Francis. *Every Day Life in the Massachusetts Bay Colony.* Boston: Society for the Preservation of New England Antiquities, 1935.

Dunkle, Robert J., and Ann S. Lainhart. *Records of the Churches of Boston.* CD-ROM. Boston: New England Historic Genealogical Society, 2002.

Early Essex County, Massachusetts, Deeds. Images of original volumes at <www.salemdeeds.com>.

English Origins of New England Families from the New England Historical and Genealogical Register. first series, 3 vols.; second series, 3 vols. Baltimore: Genealogical Publishing Company, 1984, 1985.

Essex County, Massachusetts, Probate Records, 1635–1681, 3 vols. Salem: Essex Institute, 1916–20. Available on CD-ROM with Essex County Vital Records from Search & Research.

Folsom, Samuel H., and William E. Rogers. "Index to the Probate Records of Middlesex County, Massachusetts, 1648–1871." 2-volume typescript at NEHGS. Available to NEHGS members at <www.NewEnglandAncestors.org>.

Galvin, William Francis. *Historical Data Relating to Counties, Cities, and Towns in Massachusetts*, 5th ed. Boston: New England Historic Genealogical Society, 1997.

George, Elijah. *Index to the Probate Records of the County of Suffolk, Massachusetts, from the Year 1636 to and including the Year 1893.* 3 vols. Boston: Rockwell and Churchill, 1895.

Hale, Edward Everett Jr. *Note-book Kept by Thomas Lechford, Esq., Lawyer: in Boston, Massachusetts Bay, from June 27, 1638 to July 29, 1641.* Cambridge: John Wilson and Son, 1885.

Harlow, George H. *Index to the Probate Records of the County of Worcester, Massachusetts, from July 12, 1731, to January 1, 1920,* 5 vols. Worcester, Mass.: Oliver B. Wood, 1898–1920. Series A goes through 1881. Available to NEHGS members at <www.NewEnglandAncestors.org>.

Haskell, John D. Jr. *Massachusetts, a Bibliography of its History.* Boston: G. K. Hall, 1976.

Index of Obituaries in Boston Newspapers, 1704–1800. 3 vols. Boston: G. K. Hall, 1968.

Lainhart, Ann S. *Researcher's Guide to Boston.* Boston: New England Historic Genealogical Society, 2003.

Lambert, David Allen. *A Guide to Massachusetts Cemeteries.* Boston: New England Historic Genealogical Society, 2002.

"Late Nineteenth-Century Atlases of Massachusetts Counties." Piper Publishing. CD-ROM. These maps, made from the extremely detailed 1870s Beers Atlases of Berkshire, Bristol, Essex, Franklin, Hampden, Hampshire, Middlesex, and Worcester counties are excellent resources for locating roads, waterways, and even homes of the colonial period.

Long, John H., and Gordon Den Boer. *Connecticut, Maine, Massachusetts, Rhode Island Atlas of Historical County Boundaries*. New York: Simon and Shuster, 1994.

Longver, Phillis O., and Pauline J. Oesterlin. *A Surname Guide to Massachusetts Town Histories*. Bowie, Md.: Heritage Books, 1993.

Old Maps of Northeastern Essex County, Massachusetts and *Old Maps of Southern Essex County, Massachusetts*, reproducing 1880s maps. Fryeburg: Saco Valley Printing, 1982, 1984.

Records and Files of the Quarterly Court, Essex County, Massachusetts, 1636–92. 9 vols. Salem: Essex Institute, 1911–75.

Records of the Court of Assistants of the Colony of the Massachusetts Bay, 1630–1692. 3 vols. Boston: Rockwell and Churchill Press, 1901–28.

Report of the Record Commissioners of Boston. 39 vols. Boston: Rockwell and Churchill, 1876–1909. Most of the volumes relate to the colonial period. In addition to Boston proper, it includes volumes on Charlestown, Dorchester, and Roxbury.

Records of the Suffolk County Court 1671–1680. Boston: Colonial Society of Massachusetts, 1933.

Sanborn, Melinde Lutz. *Ages from Court Records, 1636–1700: Essex, Middlesex, and Suffolk Counties, Massachusetts*. Baltimore: Genealogical Publishing Company, 2003.

———. *Lost Babes: Fornication Abstracts from Court Records, Essex County, Massachusetts, 1692 to 1745*. Derry, N.H.: the author, 1992.

———. *Essex County, Massachusetts, Probate Index, 1638–1840*. Boston: the author, 1987.

Schutz, John A. *Legislators of the Massachusetts General Court, 1691–1780: A Biographical Dictionary*. Boston: Northeastern University Press, 1997.

Shurtleff, Nathaniel B. *Records of the Governor and Company of the Massachusetts Bay in New England, 1628–1686*. 5 vols. Boston: W. White, 1853–54.

Suffolk Deeds. 14 vols. Boston: Rockwell and Churchill, city printers, 1880–1906.

Thwing, Annie Haven. *The Crooked and Narrow Streets of Boston 1630–1822*. Boston: Marshall Jones Company, 1920. Available on CD-ROM from New England Historic Genealogical Society, including "Inhabitants and Estates of the Town of Boston 1630–1800" (the augmented Thwing card file at the Massachusetts Historical Society).

Vital Records of [town], *Massachusetts, to the End of the Year 1849* [also *to the Year 1850*]. Begun by the Essex Institute and continued by the New England Historic Genealogical Society. Images on CD-ROM for the counties of Barnstable, Berkshire, Bristol, Dukes, Essex, Franklin, Hampden, Hampshire, Middlesex, Nantucket, Norfolk, Plymouth, Suffolk, and Worcester have been published by Search and Research.

Weeks, Lyman Horace, and Edwin M. Bacon. *An Historical Digest of the Provincial Press: Being a Collation of All Items of Personal and Historic Reference Relating to American Affairs Printed in the Newspapers of the Provincial Period*. Boston: Society for Americana, 1911.

Winthrop Papers, Volume IV, 1638–1644. Massachusetts Historical Society, 1944.

Wyman, Thomas Bellows. "Abstracts of Court Files of Middlesex County, Massachusetts, 1649–1675." 2-volume typescript at New England Historic Genealogical Society. Available to NEHGS members at <www.NewEnglandAncestors.org>.

New Hampshire

Copeley, William. *Index to Genealogies in New Hampshire Town Histories*. n.p.: New Hampshire Historical Society, n.d.

Evans, Helen F. *Index of References to American Women in Colonial Newspapers through 1800*. 3 vols. Bedford, N. H.: Bibliographer, 1979, 1995. All New Hampshire. Colonial references are in vols. 1 and 2.

Goss, Mrs. Charles Carpenter. *Colonial Gravestone Inscriptions in the State of New Hampshire*. Dover: Historic Activities Committee of the National Society of the Colonial Dames of America in the State of New Hampshire, 1942.

Hammond, Otis G. *Notices from the New Hampshire Gazette, 1765–1800.* Lambertville, N.J.: Hunterdon House, 1970. Otis G. and Priscilla Hammond. *Vital Records Contained in the New Hampshire Gazette from 1756 to 1800,* typescript at New Hampshire Historical Society; microfilm at Family History Library. Available to NEHGS members at <www.NewEnglandAncestors. org>.

Haskell, John D. Jr. *New Hampshire, a Bibliography of its History.* Boston: G. K. Hall, 1979.

Levermore, Charles H. *The Republic of New Haven: A History of Municipal Evolution.* Baltimore: John Hopkins University Press, 1886.

Long, John H., Gordon Den Boer, and George E. Goodridge, Jr. *New Hampshire and Vermont Atlas of Historical County Boundaries.* New York: Simon and Shuster, 1993.

Merrill, Eliphalet, and Phinehas Merrill. *Gazetteer of the State of New Hampshire.* Exeter: Norris and Co., 1817.

New Hampshire Historical Society. *Collections.* 15 vols. Concord: New Hampshire Historical Society, 1824–1939.

Noyes, Sybil; Charles Thornton Libby; and Walter Goodwin Davis. *Genealogical Dictionary of Maine and New Hampshire.* 2 vols. Portland, Me.: Southworth Press, 1928–9. Available by subscription at <www.Ancestry.com> and on CD-ROM from Family Tree Maker.

Old Maps of . . . New Hampshire, series by county, reproducing 1892 cadastral (tax) maps. Fryeburg: Saco Valley Printing, 1980s.

Pope, Charles Henry. *The Pioneers of Maine and New Hampshire, 1623 to 1660: a Descriptive List, Drawn from Records of the Colonies, Towns, Churches, Courts and Other Contemporary Sources.* Boston: the author, 1908.

Mevers, Frank C. "Consolidated Index to the Provincial and State Papers of New Hampshire," (online PDF publication, 2004) New Hampshire Division of Archives and Records Management <www. sos.nh.gov/archives>.

Provincial and State Papers of New Hampshire. 40 vols. Concord: State printer, 1867–1943.

- Boulton, Nathaniel. Volumes 1–7, Provincial Papers, primarily legislative and governmental papers from 1623–1776.
- Boulton, Nathaniel. Volumes 8 and 9, Documents and Records Relating to Towns in New Hampshire.
- Boulton, Nathaniel. Volume 10, Provincial papers from 1623–1776, including the 1773 census.
- Hammond, Otis G., and Albert Stillman Batchellor. Volumes 18–23, Provincial and State Papers from 1679–1793.
- Batchellor, Albert Stillman. Volumes 24–29, Town charters and early town documents (alphabetically by town), and the Masonian Papers, which cover towns in the Masonian patent.
- Batchellor, Albert Stillman; Henry Harrison Metcalfe; and Otis G. Hammond. Volumes 31–39. Probate records from 1635–1771.
- Hammond, Otis G. Volume 40, Court records from 1652–68.

Stearns, Ezra S. *Genealogical and Family History of the State of New Hampshire: A Record of the Achievements of her People in the Making of a Commonwealth and the Founding of a Nation.* 4 vols. New York: Lewis Publishing Co., 1908.

Towle, Laird C., and Ann N. Brown. *New Hampshire Genealogical Research Guide.* Bowie, Md.: Heritage Books, 1983.

Plymouth Colony

Plymouth Colony merged with Massachusetts in 1691; it included the modern Massachusetts counties of Plymouth, Bristol, and Barnstable.

Bangs, Jeremy Dupertis. "Pilgrim Life," in *New England Ancestors,* publication of the New England Historic Genealogical Society. A series of articles focusing on the Leiden years of the Pilgrims.

———. *Indian Deeds: Land Transactions in Plymouth Colony, 1620–1691.* Boston: New England Historic Genealogical Society, 2002.

Deetz, James, and Patricia Scott Deetz. *The Times of Their Lives: Life, Love, and Death in Plymouth Colony.* New York: W. H. Freeman, 2000. Available at libraries subscribing to <www.netlibrary.com>.

Demos, John Putnam. *A Little Commonwealth: Family Life in Plymouth Colony.* New York: Oxford University Press, 1970.

Genealogies of Mayflower Families from the New England Historical and Genealogical Register. 3 vols. Baltimore: Genealogical Publishing Company, 1985.

Konig, David Thomas. *Plymouth Church Records, 1620–1859* in *Publications of the Colonial Society of Massachusetts,* vols. 22–23, 1920. Available on CD-ROM from NEHGS.

————. *Plymouth Court Records, 1686–1859.* 16 vols. Wilmington, Del.: Michael Glazier, Inc., 1978–81. Available on CD-ROM from New England Historic Genealogical Society.

Mayflower Families in Progress. Plymouth: General Society of Mayflower Descendants. Ongoing project by various authors to review and update descendants of individual *Mayflower* passengers.

Mayflower Families through Five Generations. 21 vols. to date. Plymouth: General Society of Mayflower Descendants, 1975–. An ongoing series commonly referred to as the "5 G's" or "silver books"; compiled genealogies for *Mayflower* passengers through the fifth generation.

Peirce, Ebenezer Weaver. *Civil, Military, and Professional Lists of Plymouth and Rhode Island Colonies, Comprising Colonial, County, and Town Officers, Clergymen, Physicians and Lawyers, with Extracts from Colonial Laws Defining their Duties 1621–1700.* Boston: the author, 1881.

Roser, Susan E. *Mayflower Deeds and Probates from the Files of George Ernest Bowman at the Massachusetts Society of Mayflower Descendants.* Baltimore: Genealogical Publishing Company, 1994.

Shurtleff, Nathaniel B., and David Pulsifer. *Records of the Colony of New Plymouth in New England.* 12 vols. in 10. Boston: William White, 1855–61.

Stratton, Eugene Aubrey. *Plymouth Colony: Its History and People, 1620–1691.* Salt Lake City: Ancestry, 1986. The major scholarly study on Plymouth Colony; includes transcripts of major documents.

Willison, George F. *Saints and Strangers.* New York: Reynal and Hitchcock, 1945. A popular, easy-to-read account, but with some interpretations that are no longer accepted.

Rhode Island

Arnold, James N. *James Arnold's Tombstone Records Collection.* 32 vols. Typescript at Knight Memorial Library, Providence; microfilm at Family History Library.

———. *The Records of the Proprietors of the Narragansett, Otherwise Called the Fones Record.* Providence: Narragansett Historical Publishing, 1894.

———. *Vital Records of Rhode Island, 1636–1850, A Family Register of the People.* 21 vols. Providence: Narragansett Historical Publishing Company, 1891–1912. Volumes 13–15 index the *Providence Gazette.* Available to NEHGS members at <www.NewEnglandAncestors. org>.

Austin, John Osborne. *Genealogical Dictionary of Rhode Island.* Albany, N.Y.: Joel Munsell's Sons, 1887.

Bartlett, John Russell. *Records of the Colony of Rhode Island and Providence Plantations in New England.* 10 vols. Providence: A. C. Green, 1856–65. Available on CD-ROM from New England Historic Genealogical Society. The first seven volumes cover the colonial period.

Beaman, Alden G. *Rhode Island Vital Records, New Series.* Princeton, Mass.: the author, 1974–. Continues the efforts of Arnold.

Early Records of the Town of Portsmouth. Providence: E.L. Freeman, 1901.

Early Records of the Town of Providence. 21 vols. Providence: Snow & Farnham, city printers, 1892–1915.

Early Records of the Town of Warwick. Providence: E.A. Johnson, 1926.

Field, Edward. "Index to Providence, Rhode Island, Probate, 1646–1899" (Providence: The Providence Press, 1902). Available to NEHGS members at <www.NewEnglandAncestors.org>.

Fiske, Jane Fletcher. *Gleanings from Newport Court Files, 1659–1783.* Boxford, Mass.: the author, 1998.

———. *Rhode Island General Court of Trials, 1671–1704.* Boxford, Mass.: the author, 1998.

Genealogies of Rhode Island Families from the New England Historical and Genealogical Register. 2 vols. Baltimore: Genealogical Publishing Company, 1989.

Genealogies of Rhode Island Families from Rhode Island Periodicals. 2 vols. Baltimore: Genealogical Publishing Company, 1983.

Long, John H., and Gordon Den Boer. *Connecticut, Maine, Massachusetts, Rhode Island Atlas of Historical County Boundaries.* New York: Simon and Shuster, 1994.

MacGunnigle, Bruce Campbell. *Rhode Island Freemen, 1747–1755: A Census of Registered Voters.* Baltimore: Genealogical Publishing Company, 1977.

Morgan, Marshall; Cherry Fletcher Bamberg; and Jane Fletcher Fiske. *More Early Town Records of Warwick, Rhode Island: "The Book with Clasps" and "General Records"* Boston, Mass.: New England Historic Genealogical Society, 2001.

Peirce, Ebenezer Weaver. *Civil, Military, and Professional Lists of Plymouth and Rhode Island Colonies, Comprising Colonial, County, and Town Officers, Clergymen, Physicians and Lawyers, with Extracts from Colonial Laws Defining their Duties 1621–1700.* Boston: the author, 1881.

Rhode Island Court Records: Records of the Court of Trials of the Colony of Providence Plantations, 1647–1670. 2 vols. Providence: Rhode Island Historical Society, 1920, 1922.

Rhode Island Land Evidences 1648–1696. Providence: Rhode Island Historical Society, 1921.

Snow, Edwin M., et al. *Alphabetical Index of the Births, Marriages and Deaths Recorded in Providence: Vol. 1, 1636–1850.* 32 vols. Providence: Sidney S. Rider, 1879.

Taylor, Maureen A., and John Wood Sweet (vol. 2). *Runaways, Deserters, and Notorious Villains from Rhode Island Newspapers.* 2 vols. Camden, Me.: Picton Press, 1994. Excerpts from the *Providence Gazette* and all other Rhode Island newspapers 1762–1800.

Towle, Dorothy S. *Records of the Vice-Admiralty Court of Rhode Island, 1716–1752.* Washington, D.C.: American Historical Association, 1936.

Periodicals

Anderson, Robert Charles. *Great Migration Newsletter.* Printed or online subscription; reprint of volumes 1–10 available. New England Historic Genealogical Society (101 Newbury Street, Boston, MA 02116); <www.NewEnglandAncestors.org>. A quarterly newsletter focused on the period of the Great Migration, each issue has a focus on an early New England town, an article related to sources or methodology, and an extended listing of recent literature.

Connecticut Nutmegger [*The Nutmegger*] is a benefit of membership in the Connecticut Society of Genealogists (PO Box 435, Glastonbury, CT 06033); <www.csginc.org>.

Downeast Ancestry, privately published, 1977–93.

Genealogical Periodical Annual Index (GPAI), various editors, publishers. 1962–2000. It indexed all names (including queries) in a wide variety of genealogical publications.

Historical Collections of the Essex Institute, later *Essex Institute Historical Collections.* Essex Institute, Salem. 1859–1993.

Maine Genealogist, formerly the *Maine Seine,* is a benefit of membership in the Maine Genealogical Society (PO Box 221, Farmington, ME 04938); <www.rootsweb.com/~megs>.

Mayflower Descendant. A periodical of the Massachusetts Society of Mayflower Descendants, this journal has published Plymouth Colony records of all kinds, not just information about *Mayflower* passengers. Available on CD-ROM through volume 34 (plus additional publications) from Search and Research.

New England Historical and Genealogical Register [*The Register,* NEHGR] is a benefit of membership in the New England Historic Genealogical Society (101 Newbury Street, Boston, MA 02116); <www.NewEnglandAncestors.org>.

New England Ancestors, formerly *NEXUS,* is a benefit of membership in the New England Historic Genealogical Society (101 Newbury Street, Boston, MA 02116); <www.NewEnglandAncestors.org>.

New Hampshire Genealogical Record is a benefit of membership in the New Hampshire Society of Genealogists, Inc. (PO Box 2316,

Concord, NH 03302-2316). Volumes 1–7 #2 were published 1903–1910; publication resumed with volume 7 #3 in 1990.

New York Genealogical and Biographical Record [*The Record*, NYGBR], is a benefit of membership in the New York Genealogical and Biographical Society (122 E. 58th St., New York, NY 10022); <www.nygbs.org>. A CD-ROM of Jean D. Worden's every-name index to the *Record*, 1870–1998, is available. Images, beginning with the earliest issues, are currently being released on CD-ROM. Some articles, particularly those concerning Long Island residents, may relate to New England.

Periodical Source Index (PERSI). An enormous project of the Allen County (Fort Wayne, Indiana) Public Library, which has a substantial periodical collection. *PERSI* identifies the primary topic of each article in each publication. Approaching 2 million entries. Available by subscription from Ancestry.com and at <www. HeritageQuest.com> and on CD-ROM (2002 edition) from Ancestry.com.

Putnam's Monthly Historical Magazine, Salem Press Historical and Genealogical Magazine, and *Magazine of New England History*. Published by Eben Putnam 1890–1917. Focused on Salem, Massachusetts.

Rhode Island Genealogical Register, privately published 1978–1999. Has published abstracts of land evidences and of wills, continued over many issues; volume 16 has a cumulative index to the deceased.

Rhode Island Roots is a benefit of membership in the Rhode Island Genealogical Society (PO Box 7618, Warwick, RI 02887-7618); <www.rigensoc.org>.

The American Genealogist [TAG] is privately published (PO Box 398, Demorest, GA 30535-0398); <www.AmericanGenealogist.com>. The first eight volumes were titled *Families of Ancient New Haven*. Its current focus is primarily colonial (especially New England) and English origins.

The Genealogist [TG] is published for the American Society of Genealogists by Picton Press (PO Box 250, Rockport, ME 04856-250); <www.fasg.org>.

William and Mary Quarterly is published by the Omohundro Institute of
Early American History and Culture (College of William and Mary
and Colonial Williamsburg Foundation). Now in its third series; the
earlier series had more genealogy; the current focus is social history,
which provides contextual understanding. It is available online
through <www.JSTOR.org> through many universities.

Archives, Libraries, Historical Sites, and Societies

American Antiquarian Society, 185 Salisbury Street, Worcester, MA
01609; <www.AmericanAntiquarian.org>.

Association for Gravestone Studies, 278 Main Street, Greenfield, MA
01301; <www.GravestoneStudies.org>.

Connecticut Historical Society, 1 Elizabeth Street, Hartford CT 06105;
<www.chs.org>.

Connecticut Society of Genealogists, 175 Maple Street, East Hartford
CT (mailing address: PO Box 435, Glastonbury, CT 06033); <www.
csginc.org>.

Connecticut State Archives and Library, 231 Capitol Avenue, Hartford
CT 06106; <www.cslib.org>.

Fairbanks House (the oldest surviving timber frame house in North
America, built circa 1636). 511 East Street, Dedham, Massachusetts;
<www.FairbanksHouse.org>.

Historic Deerfield. Deerfield, Massachusetts; <www.historic-deerfield.
org/>.

Maine Genealogical Society, PO Box 221, Farmington, ME 04938;
<www.rootsweb.com/~megs>.

Maine Historical Society, 489 Congress Street, Portland, ME 04101;
<www.MaineHistory.org>.

Maine Old Cemetery Association [MOCA]. PO Box 641, Augusta, ME
04332-0641; <www.rootsweb.com/~memoca/moca.htm>.

Maine State Archives, 84 State House Station, Augusta, ME 04333;
<www.state.me.us/sos/arc>.

Massachusetts Archives, 220 Morrissey Blvd., Boston, MA 02125;
<www.state.ma.us/sec/arc/arcidx.htm>.

Massachusetts Historical Society, 1154 Boylston, Boston, MA 02215; <www.MassHist.org>.

Mayflower II. Plymouth, Massachusetts; <www.plimoth.org>.

Mystic Seaport, 75 Greenmanville Avenue, Mystic, CT 06355; <www.MysticSeaport.org>.

New England Historic Genealogical Society, 101 Newbury Street, Boston, MA 02116; <www.NewEnglandAncestors.org>. The website has an ongoing, aggressive program adding abstracts, indexes, and digital content for access by members.

New Hampshire Division of Archives and Records Management, 71 South Fruit Street, Concord, NH 03301; <www.sos.nh.gov/archives>.

New Hampshire Historical Society and Library, 30 Park Street, Concord, NH 03301-6384; <www.NHHistory.org>.

Peabody Essex Museum and Phillips Library, East India Square, Salem, MA 01970, <www.pem.org>; includes the former Essex Institute.

Plimouth Plantation, 137 Warren Avenue, Plymouth, MA 02360; <www.plimoth.org>.

Rebecca Nurse Homestead, 129 Pine Street, Danvers, MA 01923; <www.RebeccaNurse.org>.

Rhode Island Historical Society and Library, 110 Benevolent Street, Providence, RI 02906; <www.rihs.org>.

Rhode Island Genealogical Society, PO Box 7618, Warwick, RI 02887-7618); <www.rigensoc.org>.

Rhode Island State Archives, 337 Westminster Street, Providence, RI 02903; <www.state.ri.us/archives>.

Saugus Iron Works National Historic Site, Saugus, Massachusetts; <www.nps.gov/sair>.

Index

A

African Americans, population growth, 33
Andros regime, 17
Anglicans (Church of England), 29

B

Baptists, 29
blacks. *See* African Americans, population growth
broadsides, defined, 36
business records, 103–4

C

calendar
    ecclesiastical, 45–46
    Gregorian, 43–44
    Julian, 42–43
chronology, of colonial events, 117–22
Church of England (Anglicanism), 29
colleges, establishment of, 40

colonial research, defined, 1
colonies
    boundary disputes, 18
    commerce and trade in, 31–32
    in Connecticut, 13–14
    education system of, 39–41
    expansion of, 10–11
    growth of, 10–13
    late settlements, 17
    Massachusetts Bay, 9–10
    monetary system of, 46
    New Haven, 13–14
    Plymouth, 7–9
    population, growth of, 24
    postal system of, 38
    purpose of, 19
    religion in, 25–31
    transportation system of, 32
    wars and conflicts of, 20–24
colonists
    characteristics of, 6–7
    education of, 39–41
    given names of, 47
    literacy of, 41–42
    occupations of, 31–32

manuscript collections, 65–66
maps, 95
Massachusetts
    land records, 94
    local histories, 58
    military records, 100
Massachusetts Bay Colony
    government and court records, 80
    history of, 9–10
Mayflower Compact, 8
microfilmed records, 62–63
military records, 100–101
monarchs. *See* English rulers, list of
monetary system, 46
museums, using in research, 114–15

N

names, of colonists, 47
Native Americans
    conflicts with, 20–21
    relationships with, 36
naturalization records, 87–88
New England
    historic sites, 115
    northern, settlement of, 15
    population of, during colonial
      period, 24
    town model, 11
New England Confederation, 17
New Hampshire
    government and court records, 81
    land records, 94
    military records, 100
    settlement of, 15
New Haven Colony
    government and court records, 81
    history of, 13–14
newspapers, during colonial period, 36–38

O

occupations, of colonists, 31–32

P

Pequot War, 20–21
periodicals (genealogy), 58–61
Periodical Source Index (PERSI), 61
Pilgrims, in Plymouth Colony, 7–9
Plymouth Colony
    government and court records, 80
    history of, 7–9
    local histories, 58
    military records, 100
population growth, during colonial
    period, 24
postal system, 38
primer, defined, 41
private papers, 101–5
probate records, 90–92
Puritans, in Massachusetts Bay Colony,
    9–10

Q

Quakers, 29
Queen Ann's War, 22

R

records
    access to, 75–77
    business, 103–4
    cemetery, 92–93
    of counties, 86–87
    court, 79–82
    difficulties using, 74
    government, 79–82
    interpreting, 66–70
    land, 93–95
    lists, 95–100
    manuscript collections, 65–66
    military, 100–101
    naturalization, 87–88
    of schools, 41
    on microfilm, 62–63

About the Author

Patricia Law Hatcher, FASG, is a professional genealogist specializing in problem solving who has spoken at many national conferences and institutes. Her oft-migrating ancestors lived in all of the original colonies prior to 1800 and seventeen other states, presenting her with highly varied research problems and forcing her to acquire techniques and tools that help solve tough problems. In 2000, she was elected one of the fifty Fellows of the American Society of Genealogists.

She wrote the classic *Producing a Quality Family History*, published by Ancestry. Her articles have appeared in more than a dozen publications, both scholarly and popular. She was a frequent contributor to the *Ancestry Daily News*, writing more than one hundred articles for the e-newsletter, including many on problem solving and on life in early America. For *Ancestry* Magazine, she has written articles on a variety of topics, including tax records, ship building in early America, panoramic photographs, and signatures and marks. She is the editor of *The New York Genealogical and Biographical Record*; the editor of *The Pennsylvania Genealogical Magazine*; a contributing editor for the *Maine Genealogist*; a consulting editor for Newbury Street Press; the author of *Locating Your Roots—Discover Your Ancestors Using Land Records*; and has been a consulting editor for *The New England Historical and Genealogical Register*, the indexer for *The National Genealogical Society Quarterly*, and a trustee of the Association of Professional Genealogists.